Postcolonialism and Religions

Series Editors
Joseph Duggan
Postcolonial Networks
San Francisco, CA, USA

Johann Jayakiran Sebastian
United Lutheran Seminary
Philadelphia, PA, USA

The Postcolonialism and Religions series by its very name bridges the secular with the sacred through hybrid, interstitial, and contrapuntal inquiries. The series features the scholarship of indigenous scholars working at the intersections of postcolonial theories, theologies, and religions. The editors welcome authors around the world in an effort to move beyond and interrogate a historical North American and Euro-centric postcolonial studies disciplinary dominance. The series seeks to foster subaltern voices especially from Africa, Asia, Central and South America, and the liquid continent.

More information about this series at
http://www.palgrave.com/gp/series/14535

Jonathan Dunn • Heleen Joziasse
Raj Bharat Patta • Joseph Duggan
Editors

Multiple Faiths in Postcolonial Cities

Living Together after Empire

We hope you enjoy our chapter(!) – the introduction also of interest.

All love

Helena

palgrave
macmillan

Christmas 2019

Editors
Jonathan Dunn
Department of Theology & Religious
Studies, University of Chester
Chester, UK

Raj Bharat Patta
Lincoln Theological Institute
University of Manchester
Manchester, UK

Heleen Joziasse
Mara Foundation
The Hague, The Netherlands

Utrecht University
Utrecht, The Netherlands

Joseph Duggan
Postcolonial Networks
San Francisco, CA, USA

Postcolonialism and Religions
ISBN 978-3-030-17143-8   ISBN 978-3-030-17144-5   (eBook)
https://doi.org/10.1007/978-3-030-17144-5

This Palgrave Macmillan imprint is published by the registered company Springer Nature Switzerland AG
The registered company address is: Gewerbestrasse 11, 6330 Cham, Switzerland

FOREWORD

It is a pleasure to commend this collection of essays to the wide readership that it deserves. The essays presented here originate from a conference held at the Lincoln Theological Institute at the University of Manchester in May 2016. That conference, called 'Multiple Faiths in Postcolonial Cities: Living Together After Empire', brought a remarkable decade-long project to a close. Joseph Duggan, then a PhD student in Theology here at the University of Manchester, originated that project, called *Divinity After Empire*. As he developed his scholarly work in postcolonial ecclesiology, Dr Duggan decided to develop alongside it this conference project in what he would later call 'knowledge activism'. The Lincoln Theological Institute contributed to this effort and it has been a great pleasure to have been part of this work. I am delighted to see this collection of essays—the final scholarly contribution of the *Divinity After Empire* project—come to publication.

For several decades, postcolonial scholarship has flourished in the fields of the study of literature, cultural theory, history and even biblical studies. However, the impact on theology has been weaker. As R. S. Sugirtharajah noted in 2004, 'European colonialism has never been a popular subject for theological inquiry in Western discourse despite the very substantial links between the churches of Britain and the missions of the colonial world'. *Divinity After Empire* was designed to encourage Theology's engagement with postcolonial scholarship and this volume, as well as other publications from the project, indicates its success. The project has also deliberately provided occasions for interactions between postcolonial theorists and theologians. There have also been follow-on projects: the Postcolonial

Theology Network, Postcolonial Networks, a series with Palgrave Macmillan called Postcolonialism and Religions (commissioning editors, Burke Gertsenschlager and Phil Getz), and Borderless Press—all established through the tireless and enabling work of Joe Duggan. It is a remarkable story.

The first conference, also in Manchester, was held in 2008 at Joe Duggan's initiative under the title 'Church, Identities and Post/colonialism'. It was, we believe, the first conference on this theme in the UK. A presentation arising from this conference was made at the 2008 Lambeth Conference at Canterbury and conference papers were published in the *Journal of Anglican Studies* (May 2009). A second international conference was held in 2010 at United Theological Seminary, Bangalore, at the invitation of David Joy, who suggested at the first Manchester meeting that the conversations should continue. The papers from this conference have been published as *Decolonizing the Body of Christ: Theology and Theory After Empire* (edited by David Joy and Joseph Duggan, Palgrave Macmillan, 2012). A third conference, 'Story Weaving: Colonial Contexts and Postcolonial Theology' was held in Melbourne in 2012, hosted by Mark Brett and Jione Havea. Conference papers were brought together in *Colonial Contexts and Postcolonial Theologies Storyweaving in the Asia-Pacific* (Palgrave Macmillan, 2014), edited by Brett and Havea. Limuru, Kenya, was the venue in 2014 for the fourth conference, 'The Postcolonial Church: Theology, Identity and Mission', hosted by Esther Mombo at St Paul's University. The conference papers were again published, this time with Borderless Press: *The Postcolonial Church: Bible, Theology, and Mission* (2016), edited by Mombo, R. S. Wafula and Joseph Wandera. The May 2016 conference was the fifth and last of the series and, in a nice piece of symmetry, brought the project back to Manchester from where it began nearly a decade earlier.

The 2016 conference was a lively occasion and Manchester in all its diversity proved to be a good location. The conference rubric included the following comment: Colonial powers bring their religion with them and often this religion becomes an instrument of rule. When empires fall, the residue of imperial suspicion lingers. When colonial powers beat a retreat, older religious resentments and new tensions may emerge. We hear daily news reports in cities around the world about violent clashes between Christians and Muslims, Buddhists and Muslims, Shia and Sunnis, Catholics and Protestants and more.

Thereafter, the conference posed a series of questions:

- Why have we not as frequently heard of postcolonial cities where people of multiple faiths peacefully coexist?
- How do people of goodwill organise for cities based on multiplicity of identities, languages, religions and shared public space?
- What role do theologians and theorists have in fostering collaborative spaces for faith communities to coexist in ways that work for justice for all people?
- How are the misuses of religion addressed?
- How do our religions and theologies need to change to foster people of multiple faiths living side by side after empire?

A range of responses to these questions is to be found in the essays that follow. The editors of this volume—the last in the *Divinity After Empire* series—have done an excellent job in presenting these and are warmly to be thanked for their hard work. Their Introduction provides a summary of each essay and I shall not intrude on that work. I would, however, like to commend these essays as part of *Divinity After Empire*'s effort to encourage the engagement by Theology with the postcolonial. Together with the editors of all the volumes, it is to Joe Duggan that we owe thanks that this conversation has proceeded as far as it has. LTI has been delighted to be a part of it, and looks forward to further collaboration in this important work. I hope that you find the arguments, analyses and insights in the following pages helpful to your scholarship and wider work.

Director, Lincoln Theological Institute   Peter Manley Scott
The University of Manchester

ACKNOWLEDGEMENTS

The editors would like to acknowledge the vital role played by the Lincoln Theological Institute (LTI), University of Manchester, and in particular its director Peter Manley Scott, in facilitating the production of this volume and the conference which birthed it. This sits within LTIs wider contribution to the work of promoting and developing the type of conversations which this volume seeks to encourage. Indeed, three of the editors have been among the many early career researchers who have benefited from LTI's proactive approach and distinctive research environment, in particular Peter Scott's stimulating doctoral supervision.

Special thanks also go to those who participated in the conference, in particular those who have developed their conference papers into the chapters of this volume, for their openness, effort and patience.

We wish to express our appreciation of the way in which Amy Invernizzi and Phil Getz at Palgrave Macmillan have guided and supported three first-time editors through the submission process.

We also acknowledge the support of the series editors, J. Jayakiran Sebastian and Joe Duggan, without which this volume would not have been published. Heleen, Jonathan and Raj would also like to acknowledge our deepest gratitude to Joe, for his mentorship throughout the production of this volume, through difficult circumstances.

Finally, we remember with gratitude Stefani Schatz (Joe's spouse). We hope that this volume will be a fitting memorial to her commitment to knowledge activism.

CONTENTS

Notes on Contributors

Phil Barton worked in local environmental regeneration for 35 years in Manchester, North West England, and throughout the UK until 2015, most recently as Chief Executive of Keep Britain Tidy. During that time he worked extensively across sectors—central and local government, business, NGOs, educational, faith and local communities. He is undertaking a Masters in Art and Science at Central Saint Martins in London.

Terry Biddington is Dean of Spiritual Life and Lecturer in Practical Theology at the University of Winchester and associate member of staff at the Manchester University Centre for the History of Science, Technology and Medicine. He was previously Co-ordinating and Anglican Chaplain for the Manchester Higher Education Community.

Elaine Bishop emigrated to Manchester as a result of marriage, in 1972, from California where she was a high school English teacher. She has been living on the same Manchester street since 1979 and worked in Manchester's Ethnic Minority Achievement Service as a teacher in local primary schools for 16 years. Since retirement, she has been interested in community cohesion and was a co-founder of her neighbourhood Residents' Association in 2009. She is Secretary of the Association.

C. I. David Joy is a presbyter of the Church of South India, South Kerala Diocese; he is a professor, teaching New Testament, at the United Theological College, Bangalore. He is also the liaison for India of

SBL-ICI (Society of Biblical Literature-International Cooperation Initiative). His recent books include *Christology: Re-visited: Profiles and Prospects* (2007), *Mark and Its Subalterns: A Hermeneutical Paradigm for a Postcolonial Context* (2008), *Not by the Might but by the Spirit* (2008), and *Kurisile Rithubhedangal* (TTF, 2009), *Kurisithe Dhyanavazhikal* (CSS, 2012), *1 and 2 Peter: A Commentary* (2012), *Hermeneutics: Foundations and New Trends* (2012) and *Kurisnte Dhyanavazhikal* (CSS, 2012). His recent edited volumes include *Biblical Theology* (2008), *Transforming Praxis* (2008), *Bible and Hermeneutics* (2010), co-edited along with Joseph Duggan, *Decolonizing the Body of Christ: Theology and Theory After Empire?* (Palgrave Macmillan, 2012), *Overlooked Voices: A Postcolonial Indian Quest* (2015), and co-edited with Mohan Larbeer, *Journeys into the Deep: Hermeneutical Patterns of M. M. Thomas* (2016).

Jonathan Dunn is Lecturer in Theological Ethics at the University of Chester. He was the Mark Gibbs Doctoral Student (2015–2018) at the Lincoln Theological Institute, University of Manchester. He is a former licentiate minister of the Presbyterian Church in Ireland.

Heleen Joziasse has a Bachelor of Theology and a Masters of Theology from the Free University, Amsterdam, The Netherlands. Since 1994, she is an ordained minister in the Protestant Church in The Netherlands. From 1997–1999, she worked as a research assistant at the Christian Study Centre, Rawalpindi, Pakistan, and between 2009–2014, she joined St Paul's University, Limuru, Kenya, in the faculty of Theology and taught Systematic Theology and Gender Studies. She is a PhD candidate (University of Utrecht, The Netherlands) in the area of African women's Christologies and Gender. She coordinates a network of international and migrant churches in The Hague: a project of Mara Foundation.

Helena Mary Kettleborough *Wandering Scholar*, delivers workshops on growing hopeful futures to a range of audiences, drawing on community development, action research, ecology, cosmology and social justice. Teaching at Manchester Metropolitan University (MMU), she was awarded her PhD from Lancaster Business School. Kettleborough's career was as a senior manager in Local Authorities delivering community development and neighbourhood regeneration services within the North West of England. For the last decade, she has volunteered with Elaine, her Civil Partner Phil and neighbours to improve their locality.

Esther Mombo holds a Bachelor of Divinity from St Paul's University in Limuru, Kenya, a Masters in Philosophy from Trinity College, Dublin, Ireland, a PhD from Edinburgh, Scotland, and an honorary PhD from Virginia Theological Seminary. She has worked as a theological educator in St Paul's Theological College and St Paul's United Theological College now St Paul's University (SPU). Her areas of teaching include church history, gender, HIV and AIDS, and African women's theology. As a member of the Circle, she has worked extensively to support women in both theological education and ministry in the church. After having served as Deputy Vice Chancellor (Academics) at SPU, she is Director International Partnerships and Alumni Relations at SPU.

Raj Bharat Patta is an ordained minister of the Andhra Evangelical Lutheran Church (AELC) in India, and is serving as an authorised Methodist minister at the Stockport Circuit in Greater Manchester, England. He received his PhD in Religion and Theology from the University of Manchester in 2018.

Peter Manley Scott is Samuel Ferguson Professor of Applied Theology and Director of the Lincoln Theological Institute at the University of Manchester. He is author of *Theology, Ideology and Liberation* (1994), *A Political Theology of Nature* (2003), *Anti-human Theology: Nature, Technology and the Postnatural* (2010), and numerous articles, and co-editor of the *Blackwell Companion to Political Theology* (2004; second edition 2018), *Future Perfect* (2006), *Re-moralising Britain?* (2009), *Nature, Space and the Sacred* (2009), *Systematic Theology and Climate Change* (2014) and *At Home in the Future* (2016). He is a member of the Center of Theological Inquiry (Princeton, USA), and part of its enquiry in Astrobiology, Chair of the European Forum for the Study of Religion and the Environment, and Co-Investigator for the ESRC-funded project 'Life on the Breadline: Christianity, Poverty and Politics in the 21st Century City'.

Chris Shannahan is Assistant Professor of Political Theology at the Centre for Trust, Peace and Social Relations at Coventry University. Before joining Coventry University he taught at the University of Manchester and the University of Birmingham. His grassroots experience as the head of Religious Education in a large East London Secondary School, a youth worker in London and Trenchtown, Jamaica, a Methodist

Mminister in inner-city London and Birmingham and a community organiser provided the grounding for his research and the basis of his 2008 PhD, within which he developed the first critical analysis of British urban theology. His first monograph, *Voices from the Borderland* (2010), provided a critical analysis of British urban theology since its inception in the early 1970s and his second book, *A Theology of Community Organizing* (2014), provided the first systematic theological analysis of broad-based community organising. His research focuses on contemporary Christian approaches to poverty in post-financial crash Britain and on Christianity, 'race' and racism in the USA and the UK.

LIST OF FIGURES

LIST OF TABLES

CHAPTER 1

Introduction

Jonathan Dunn, Heleen Joziasse, and Raj Bharat Patta

The Continuing Relevance of 'Living Together After Empire'

The chapters in this volume were presented in May 2016 at a conference at the University of Manchester, entitled 'Multiple Faiths in postcolonial cities: Living together after Empire'. On 22 May 2017, one year after the Manchester conference, people were startled by a terrorist attack, which took place at the end of a concert of a teen pop-idol, Ariana Grande, in the Manchester Arena. The attack claimed 23 lives (including the attacker)

J. Dunn (✉)
Department of Theology & Religious Studies, University of Chester, Chester, UK
e-mail: j.dunn@chester.ac.uk

H. Joziasse
Mara Foundation, The Hague, The Netherlands

Utrecht University, Utrecht, The Netherlands

R. B. Patta
Lincoln Theological Institute, University of Manchester, Manchester, UK

© The Author(s) 2019
J. Dunn et al. (eds.), *Multiple Faiths in Postcolonial Cities*, Postcolonialism and Religions,
https://doi.org/10.1007/978-3-030-17144-5_1

1

and wounded many people.[1] Two days later, religious leaders—Christians, Muslims, Jews, Hindus and leaders of other religious denominations—rallied and showed unity, giving a powerful message of resilience, demonstrating the strength of multiple faiths joining together to address and defeat the forces of hatred and prejudice.[2] These events point to both the continued challenges of living together after empire faced in many postcolonial cities, and the attempts by faith communities to meet those challenges. The theme of the 2016 conference and this volume, 'Living together after empire', addresses concerns which are evidently faced in many urban contexts, and not exclusively those of Europe and Northern America. Indeed, African capitals, such as Nairobi and Bamako, have also witnessed terrorist attacks, as have Dhaka and Jakarta, to name but a few. This project then, attempts to engage with these concerns and to resource the meeting of the challenges of living together 'after empire'.

While power structures of 'after empire societies' are tested, and often symbols of Western hegemony are targeted, religious communities, usually represented by male leaders, speak powerful words to refute diversifying powers and show a resilient society. In doing so, religious communities reveal themselves to be able to respond to these challenges in a way which offers hope of resolution. The revelation of this resilience contests dominant narratives which problematize religious belief in its diverse forms in a way which, at the least, implies that religious belief makes living together more difficult. These responses also highlight and test the limits which political agendas place on the expression of religious belief. For, while in formerly Christian but presently secular or post-secular societies, religious

---

[1] The conference from which this volume has emerged was the fifth and final meeting in the 'Divinity after Empire' series of international conferences. Previous conferences were held on 'Identities and Post/colonialism', 1–2 May 2008, at the University of Manchester, with papers subsequently published in the *Journal of Anglican Studies*, 7(1), 2009; 'Decolonizing the Body of Christ: Theology and Theory After Empire', January 2010, at the United Theological Seminary, Bangalore with papers subsequently published as *Decolonizing the Body of Christ: Theology and Theory After Empire* (ed. David Joy and Joseph Duggan, New York, NY: Palgrave Macmillan, 2012); 'Story Weaving: Colonial Contexts and Postcolonial Theology', 24–26 January, 2012, Melbourne, Australia; 'The Postcolonial Church: Theology, Identity and Mission', 28–30 May 2014, Limuru, Kenya, with papers subsequently published as *The Postcolonial Church: Bible, Theology and Mission* (ed. R.S. Wafula, Esther Mombo, and Joseph Wandera, Alameda, CA: Borderless Press, 2016).

[2] See, for example, http://metro.co.uk/2017/05/24/bishop-and-imam-hold-hands-at-vigil-to-remember-manchester-terror-attack-victims-6659947/#ixzz4p5AJ2EKu retrieved 7-8-2017.

expressions of different faith communities are foregrounded, especially in times of 'personal crises', this foregrounding comes with restrictions on religious expressions, which force religious actors (or people of faith) to express their faith in a politically correct way.

The nature and scale of these restrictions on religious expression vary across the many contexts touched upon by this volume. Indeed, this volume is offered with an awareness of these variances and other significant differences between the contexts it covers. For while change is apparently in the air in one context, in another it remains elusive, despite being sought-after and mistakenly perceived. For the people of Manchester, and across a British context still struck by the collapse of an empire, change appears imminent, and the prospect is often met with a sense of foreboding. The vote in favour of 'Brexit' on 23 June 2016 has been widely interpreted as signalling a turn away from the rest of the world. With concerns over immigration, particularly the economic migration of people from Eastern Europe, apparently motivating many among the narrow majority who voted to quit the European Union, such an interpretation appears compelling. In contrast to the perception of imminent change in that context, in countries which have had to endure both conquest by colonial entities such as Britain, and Western cultural hegemony, there are no overt signs of change nor are there clear signs of a new 'era': Power relations continue, while cultural and economic hegemony feeds migration. However, a post-colonial theory and theology reveals counter hegemonic ideas and practices. This is, for instance, the case in a Kenyan context: Various religions and religious expressions are integrated in public life, and in a context of marginality, agency is used to respond to religious and cultural hegemony. So, it is in the Indian context, where caste epistemologies dominate the public sphere, Dalits and such oppressed communities have been contesting such epistemologies and have been engaging in alternative visions of public spheres.

THE PROBLEMATIC IDEA OF 'AFTER EMPIRE'

In reflecting on attacks such as those in Manchester and elsewhere, a post-colonial approach raises pressing questions. Not least, that of whether these attacks are symptomatic of life after empire, or whether this deathly violence was in fact targeting empire. Indeed, the posing of this question points to the existence of a prior question, a question which continues to be at the heart of post-colonial studies: Are we actually living after empire or are we still witnessing empire, clothed in the garments of globalization?

The question of whether empire can be consigned to history, or remains very much alive under new guises, persists. Indeed, it is the persistence of this question, and its necessary relevance and centrality for post-colonial studies, which brings an interrogative dimension to this volume's title, 'Living together after empire?' This volume, and the conference which gave rise to it, has proceeded on the basis that the death of empire cannot be assumed. To some extent, the question *are we* "living after empire"?' hangs over every attempt to explore and imagine life after empire.

What exactly the 'post' of post-colonial denotes and how it relates to the notion of living *after* empire are questions which many working within this field have attempted to address. Among them is the Zimbabwean theologian, Edward Antonio, who argues that 'post' literally designates an 'after' and intimates a real 'beyond'. Hence, post-colonial theory seems to point at something about, or gestures to a possibility of, the end of formal colonialism and its political and cultural aftermath. Yet, Antonio also recognizes that globalization is experienced, especially in the formerly colonized countries and by the people who belonged to these countries, as a continuing form of colonialism; globalization iterates, repeats and reproduces the social, economic and cultural imbalances which once characterized imperial rule. Notwithstanding this observation, Antonio holds that without speaking of 'after' or post, it is not possible to locate the possibility of re-describing new power relationships. Hence, to talk about 'post' enables one to take seriously power relations in the past and in the present.[3] Therefore, in favour of the 'after' and post-colonial theory, he holds:

> To deny any division between the 'before' and 'after' of colonial time in the name of political sensitivity is not only to freeze colonial relations in the synchronic space of an ever present domination, it is also, in the end, to display the most condescending political insensitivity. Does not such a denial privilege the colonial by insinuating its eternity?[4]

Moreover, Antonio states that the denial of the 'after' in the 'post' of post-colonialism would imply a freezing of the agency of the colonially subjugated, leaving no space for possible transformation. As a theologian, furthermore, he argues that religion has always been constitutively central

---

[3] Edward P. Antonio, "Introduction: Inculturation and Postcolonial Discourse", in *Society and Politics in Africa: Inculturation and Postcolonial Discourse in African Theology* (New York: Peter Lang, 2006), 4–5.

[4] Ibid., 7.

to colonial and post-colonial relationships and therefore the post-colonial or the post-colony is structured by the religious imaginary.[5]

This project employs a contested epistemology, with oppositional knowledge emerging from the de-colonial sites. Deconstructive hermeneutical epistemologies are foregrounded out of an awareness of a further objection to post-colonial theory, and the use of 'after': This theory is mostly developed in the Western academy in Europe and North America. As such, it privileges the disciplinary practices associated with the history of Western power, for example, ignoring indigenous worldviews, reducing the past of the colonized as if nothing existed before colonization and being the elitist endeavour of a male, Anglo-American middle class. The conversations developed in our conference, and encapsulated in this volume, have been conducted in the context of this ongoing debate. While recognizing the difficulties inherent in the 'after' of the title, initially recognized through the application of a question mark, our use of the word 'after' denotes a refusal to deny or restrict the transformed and transforming agency of those empire has sought to marginalize. However, by not mentioning a question mark after 'living after empire', this volume aims to contest all forms of discourses of empire and strives for just and inclusive societies. Like the conference, this volume of essays contends that living after empire is not only a political, but also a theological concern. The challenges involved in living together after empire can only be understood fully, and met appropriately, when its theological dimensions, and their interaction with the political, are recognized. As such, it contests the restriction of religious expressions imposed by political agendas.

The Challenge of Continuing Urbanization

It is in the context of ever expanding 'neo-urban public spheres' that our project of "Living together after Empire: Multiple Faiths in Post-Colonial Cities" has evolved to interrogate, theologically and contextually, the voices of faith that emerge from post-colonial cities. The self-conscious use of the term 'after Empire', discussed above, also refers to the fluidity inherent in many current contexts and the challenges posed within such flux. The contribution of rapid urbanization, a by-product of globalization, is foremost among the factors driving such changes. This volume draws attention to this process and notes its roots in the 'colonial'. There is a focus too, on the widening of the territory and functionality of urban spheres;

---

[5] Ibid., 9.

cities have changed from small and medium cities to greater cities and mega cities. With the advent of neo-liberal economic changes, cities in, for instance, today's India are renamed as 'Greater Hyderabad', 'Greater Noida', 'Navi Mumbai' and so on. The borders of the neighbouring villages are erased to be accommodated into mega cities. With the expansion of cities, the so-called neo-urban public spheres are ever widening. Several chapters in this volume highlight the challenges of living after empire in these widening urban public spheres.

With urbanization, there has been an increase of migration from rural villages into cities in search of new jobs created by globalization projects. The mantra of globalization being only profit, only those who fit the parameters are given jobs. The social consequences of this trend are evident, not least in the way cities have become hubs of unemployment and under-employment. Furthermore, a trans-rural ethos has been brought into this neo-urban public sphere. On the one hand, the rural migrants that come into these urban spaces are struggling to cope with the urban realities and, on the other, there is a vibrancy of multiple identities that are forged and foraged giving rise to hybrid identities. It is this struggle to live between their rurality and the given neo-urbanity which projects the liminality of new identities. The struggle to live among erased village boundaries and newly drawn cities constitutes trans-rurality. This in-between-ness defines the trans-rural characteristic of the neo-urban public spheres. The cosmopolitan culture in these neo-urban public spheres is dismissive of rural lifestyles and tries to exclude them from the 'life-world' of the cities. A further sense of living 'in between' arises from the establishment of culturally segregated neighbourhoods, inhabited by people from the same tribe or nationality. At the same time in the city, a multiplicity of communal identities is constituted which often transcends ethnic boundaries. This volume attempts to keep alive the aspirations of the 'rural' in the 'trans-rural' public spheres, affirming life outside of 'urban-global' spaces.

Harnessing a Contested Epistemology and Deconstructive Hermeneutics

In a previous book produced by the Post-colonial Network, the editors gave an overview of developments of post-colonial theory and theology on the African continent. They signalled the dearth of African engagement with post-colonial theory in general, and with biblical and theological readings in particular.[6] Furthermore, they looked for reasons why post-colonial theology is not enthusiastically embraced on the African continent.[7] Should it be concluded that the use of a post-colonial reading lens to critique coloniality and misuse of power does not fit within the Majority scholarly world? Or could it be that a critique of coloniality and hegemony is intrinsic to African as well as other liberation and feminist theologies, and that post-colonial lenses focus too much on the post-secular contexts of the Western world? Hence, another effort is needed to make post-colonial discourse applicable for those who suffer most from coloniality and hierarchy, and whose reality was a multi-faith context from the onset of missionary endeavour. This effort must translate the analyses offered by post-colonial theory to a Majority World which is inherently a multi-faith world.

Concentrating on the theological application of post-colonial theory, Robert Heaney, in 'From Historical to Critical Post-Colonial Theology', explores the relation of post-colonial theology and theology that emerged in historically colonial situations, and discusses the works of two prominent Kenyan theologians, John Mbiti and Jesse Mugambe.[8] Heaney defines the goal of post-colonial theology as 'theological decolonization' and illuminates:

> Processes of theological decolonization seek to unveil oppression and suppression in theological discourses and theologies. They seek to disrupt dominant perspectives or the perspectives of the dominant in terms, for example, of biblical readings, doctrinal formulations, and church practices. They foreground the hybrid nature of Christianity and readings of Christian doctrines, traditions, and histories. In providing such counter-discourses, theological decolonization decenters the "authority" or "normality" of so-called Western assumptions and discourses.[9]

The two main objectives of the post-colonial theological enterprise, identified by Heaney, are promoting the theological agency of marginalized

---

[6] R. S. Wafula, Esther Mombo, and Joseph Wandera, eds., *The Postcolonial Church: Bible, Theology, and Mission* (Alameda, CA: Borderless Press, 2016).

[7] See: Ibid., xxiii–xxxv.

[8] Robert S. Heaney, *From Historical to Critical Post-Colonial Theology: The Contribution of John S. Mbiti and Jesse N. K. Mugambi* (Eugene: Wipf and Stock Publishers, 2015).

[9] Ibid., 30.

peoples and developing hybridized forms of theology.[10] These attest to the resistance of theological hegemony, resistance which is intrinsically woven into the contributions of this publication.

In his article, "The Idea of India: Derivative, Desi and Beyond", Gopal Guru explains the category 'beyond' which is helpful in our discussion here.[11] Firstly, he explains that the category 'beyond' refers to thinking 'which is pushed beneath and beyond the public imagination'. In other words, to invoke the category 'beyond' India, is also to invoke the contested epistemologies which have been pushed outside of the hegemonic epistemologies of India, which is to say, the caste epistemology. Secondly, Guru's category of 'beyond' is different in style and structure, for it 'expresses dissonance, difference and defiance' and disrupts hegemonic ideas. This volume follows Guru in understanding 'after' as 'beyond'. As such it seeks to interrupt hegemonic thought, like that of caste, by employing 'dissonance, difference and defiance' to the very idea of 'knowledge (from empire) is power and power is knowledge.' Thirdly, in the category of 'beyond', Guru explains that this concept brings in the real, which according to him brings 'untouchability' as 'un-thought' into reflection. Similarly, this volume brings to light the reality of marginality, giving theological voice to the 'un-thought' in the transnational, trans-rural public sphere. Fourthly, Guru explains that the concept of 'beyond', as an articulation of the margins, communicating in language that is viewed negatively, even considered grotesque, by hegemonic thought. This volume has this element of grotesque language, where protest and praise share in mutual accountability. Finally, 'beyond' is a category which is in search of an 'alternative normative ideal', for the collection of chapters in this volume deconstructs the hegemonic universal ideals.

Empire has nurtured a colonial episteme, and the language of faiths has succumbed to it by articulating its faith narratives in the logic of colonial episteme. Indeed, the very conceptualisation of 'divine as transcendental' stands as an example of how readily religious discourse has assumed colonial logic. This project self-consciously harnesses a contested epistemology to challenge such dominant paradigms and meta-narratives. It does so, not least, by de-enveloping the knowledge forms of those on the margins and

[10] Heaney, *From Historical to Critical Post-Colonial Theology*, 30.
[11] Gopal Guru, "The Idea of India: Derivative, Desi and Beyond", *Economic & Political Weekly* 46, no. 37 (2011): 36–42.

their micro-narratives. To this end, the current volume continues to cultivate deconstructive hermeneutics, pushing diverse perspectives to the fore. 'Living together after empire' is, therefore, a space where 'the self' and 'the other' are radically re-ordered and re-interrogated. It is a space where texts are interpreted using the tools of deconstruction, in full recognition that to use deconstructive hermeneutics, constitutes political activity. Here is a space where the voices of the margins are invited to find relevance and immediacy.

From a leading post-colonial feminist perspective, given by Kwok Pui-lan, the identification of marginalized agency is one of the characteristics of post-colonial theologies, while imagination is one of the key methods which is able to contest Western hegemonic thinking. This imagining, according to Kwok Pui-lan, is historical: by hearing, for example, the voices of marginalized women, dialogically; by problematizing the liberal notion of diversity and recognizing asymmetrical power relations; and by undermining the assumptions that Christianity is normatively Western.[12] Behind this method of imagination is the endeavour to critique modern thought with its 'discrete and mutually exclusive categories'.[13] Resistance against dualistic thinking is a central notion in post-colonial theologizing: a method to unveil subjugation and Western hegemony and unravel marginalized agency is to start with the lived experience of plural identities of colonialism and neo-colonialism (black, white, oppressed, oppressor).[14] The focus on the marginalized experiences of women, and, most severely, the experience of colonized women, is a final concretization of the post-colonial theological programme.[15] Several of the contributions to this volume represent efforts to develop post-colonial discourse in this direction.

Engaging with Public Theology

This volume also serves to highlight the growing interaction between post-colonial methods and theology. The potential interplay between these approaches is demonstrated in several contributions to this volume

---

[12] Ibid., 24. Heaney refers to Kwok, *Postcolonial Imagination and Feminist Theology*, 22, 29–51.

[13] Ibid., 28.

[14] Ibid., 29. Scholars such as Keller, Nausner and Rivera start with the lived experiences.

[15] Ibid. Kwok identifies the ongoing subjugation and eurocentrism in theology, which marginalizes the experiences of women and, most severely, the experience of colonized women.

which approach their contexts from a shared understanding of public theology. On the one hand, public theology is understood as God-talk where faith seeks its relevance in the public, and, on the other hand, as a public discourse where the "public" is interrogated by faith. It is also, as such, the holding together of both these poles in a creative tension. This volume suggests that multiple faiths in post-colonial cities can be heard and accommodated through such public theological parameters. Multiple faiths today face challenges from post-secularism on the one hand and religious fundamentalism on the other hand, and do so in a post-colonial context. In an era seemingly defined by 'post-truth' contexts, there has been a revival of religion in the public sphere; a revival which contests all forms of privatization of faiths. Life after Empire finds its fecundity in public theology, for public theology critically engages with notions of empire, trying to find subversive and subaltern forms of knowledge in opposition to its colonial and empire forms.

This type of engagement, with its resultant voicing of oppositional knowledge, is exemplified by Paul S. Chung's discussion of the future of Reformation Theology in Asia. In the course of that work, Chung proposes that a 'postcolonial reading of Reformation' provides a new entry in the critique of the 'imperialization of Reformation theology', an imperialization which has been used for the service of the powerful in the churches. It is an understanding of post-colonial public theology which aids our discourses here. He further says,

> In dialogue with Reformation theology, a theological project of incultura-
> tion entails prophetic-hermeneutical reasoning in revealing and clarifying
> emancipatory and constructive values inherent in Asian religions and cul-
> tures. It archeologically focusses on what has been subjugated and fore-
> closed in the study of cultures and religions regarding the irregular side of
> history, society and church. It is undertaken in terms of anamnestic reason-
> ing in dangerous and subversive remembrance upon Jesus' socio-biography
> with his people.[16]

Chung qualifies the inculturation project by emphasizing the forgotten, subjugated and foreclosed cultures side-lined by history, society and culture, for which subaltern cultures and cultural resources are part of those subjugated knowledge forms. This inculturation approach is by no

---

[16] Paul S. Chung, *Postcolonial Public Theology: Faith, Scientific Rationality and Prophetic Dialogue* (Eugene: Cascade Books, 2016) p. 40.

means limited to Asian contexts, but, as the previously mentioned work of Antonio suggests, is also prominent in African contexts.[17] Thus, living after empire is, in its post-colonial engagement with local subjugated epistemes, de-constructing imperialistic and colonial episteme. For that reason, this theological book project is needed.

Overview of the Volume

Our volume is organized in two sections, each with a slightly different focus. The first section includes contributions which highlight ongoing efforts by people of multiple faiths to live together within their contexts. The initiatives in focus include the efforts of a neighbourhood in urban Manchester to live together as people of multiple faiths, the array of attempts at creating multi-faith spaces for worship across the globe, and attempts to commemorate divisive conflict together in Northern Ireland. The second section is dedicated to work which begins with particular post-colonial methods and utilizes these to illuminate pressing issues within specific contexts.

Section One

In 'Collecting Stories of a Manchester Street, Living Together as People of MultiFaiths', Helena Mary Kettleborough, Phil Barton and Elaine Bishop begin this volume with a considered portrait of social reality in their neighbourhood within contemporary post-colonial Manchester. Their vivid account of neighbours living together as people of multi-faiths within a contemporary urban setting further contests received notions about multi-culturalism in this context.

The ability of the neighbours of Tree Grove to meet the challenges of living together as people of multi-faiths in a post-colonial city also stands in contrast to some of the attempts at facilitating multi-faith spaces illuminated by the comprehensive survey offered by Terry Biddington in his chapter, 'Multifaith Space: Religious Accommodation in Postcolonial Public Space?' This extensive examination of examples of multi-faith spaces highlights the positive potential of such spaces for development, while at the same time illuminating the restrictions under which they come into being and function.

---

[17] Antonio, "Introduction: Inculturation and Postcolonial Discourse".

In 'Remembering Together: Co-Memoration in Northern Ireland', Jonathan Dunn examines the challenge of remembering together through the lens of a Moltmannian public theology, in an attempt to renew debate surrounding the commemoration of conflict in this context. In a post-colonial vein, the chapter explores the exclusionary potential of physical symbols and liturgical approaches, and emphasizes the perspectives of those marginalized by their experience of commemoration within worshipping communities.

SECTION TWO

David Joy's, 'A Postcolonial Ethnographic Reading of Migrant/Refugee Faith Communities in Bengaluru', opens the second section of this volume by charting the extent and impact of neo-urbanization in an Indian context. Doing so by way of an ethnographic reading of these faith communities, David Joy demonstrates the potential of this particular methodology to illuminate the stories of ordinary men and women.

Heleen Joziasse and Esther Mombo's chapter, 'Worshipping God in a Mabati Church: Bishop Jane Akoth's Leadership in the African Israel Nineveh Church', also draws attention to the effects of urbanization. Their chapter not only illustrates the particular effects of urbanization on women's leadership in a Kenyan church in the semi-informal settlements of Kayole and Matopeni, in Nairobi, Kenya but also, significantly, provides an example of the focus on marginalized experiences of colonized women which is indispensable to the post-colonial theological programme. Their insight into the agency in the leadership of Bishop Jane Akoth in contrast to her marginalized experience, as a woman in the African Israel Nineveh Church, is presented as proof of a hybridized theology which destabilizes Western forms of hegemony and African patriarchal hegemony.

In 'Discipleship as Living out Baptism: A Dalit Public Engagement with Theology of Bonhoeffer', Raj Bharat Patta explores notions of 'public' in the context of Dalit Christian reality, through engaging with Bonhoeffer's understanding of discipleship as the living out of baptism, paving a way towards a public theological conversation.

Drawing this section to a close, Chris Shannahan's contribution, 'Immanuel Kant Believed in Zombies: Multiculturalism and Spirituality in the Postcolonial City', critiques still pervasive concepts of multi-culturalism which problematize diversity, primarily in a British context. His chapter contends that the political and academic debate surrounding multi-

Fig. 1.1 Conference Participants, from left to right: Farah Sattar, David Joy, Ahmed Ali, Rev. Stefani Schatz, Helen Glaizner, Robena Ahmed, Sally Foxall, Heleen Joziasse, Dennis Chisunka, Rashid Ahmed (holding grandson), Anandi Ramamurthy, Wal Singh, Peter Scott, Helena Kettleborough, Jill Singh, Esther Mombo, Sophie Flieshman, Joe Duggan, Helen Bishop, Jonathan Dunn, Anderson Jeremiah, Raj Patta

culturalism has become a zombie discourse that fails to reflect social reality of contemporary post-colonial cities.

The phrase, 'Living together after Empire', and its subtext 'afterlives in the Empire', may well be filled with a sort of ambiguity, for the episteme of coloniality has taken over lives in the Empire by conditioning the language of God-talk to serve the interests of dominant communities. This volume therefore, ventures and adventures in liberating narratives and faith perspectives from such colonial episteme, where the silenced and forgotten voices speak with courage. In fact 'living after empire(s)' is a challenging task today that calls for a deeper commitment for the transformation of our society, and this volume provides a lead towards that direction (Fig. 1.1).

CHAPTER 2

Collecting Stories of a Manchester Street, Living Together as People of Multi-Faiths

Helena Mary Kettleborough, Phil Barton, and Elaine Bishop

INTRODUCTION

In this chapter, we will be exploring how residents live together on a street in inner-city Manchester located in a deprived neighbourhood in the UK: how people from across the globe—including Pakistan, Iran, Germany, France, Ireland, Wales, Somalia, USA, Bangladesh—and Lancashire and London—live harmoniously together.[1]

---

[1] The 'Stories on our Street' project seeks to respect the confidentiality of participants and residents. To this end, the authors have changed the names of the streets in this chapter.

Rusholme was in the top 31%–40% of the most deprived neighbourhoods in England, 9854 to 13,137, out of a total of 32,844 Lower Super Output Areas in the Index of Multiple Deprivation (Manchester City Council, 2015) prior to boundary changes in 2018.

H. M. Kettleborough (✉)
Department of Strategy, Enterprise and Sustainability, Manchester Metropolitan University Business School, Manchester, UK
e-mail: h.kettleborough@mmu.ac.uk

P. Barton • E. Bishop
Centre for Connected Practice & Secretary, Residents Group, Manchester, UK

© The Author(s) 2019
J. Dunn et al. (eds.), *Multiple Faiths in Postcolonial Cities*, Postcolonialism and Religions,
https://doi.org/10.1007/978-3-030-17144-5_2

15

First occupied in the first decade of the nineteenth century, Tree Grove is in the Rusholme district of inner south Manchester close to the famous Curry Mile, the Royal Infirmary and the University of Manchester. It is near the Victoria Park estate of large nineteenth-century houses to the north, terraced housing to the east and west and more upmarket housing to the south. This part of Manchester is an unusual patchwork of areas of decline and gentrification, poverty and middle-class, parks and tight knit streets.[2]

In this chapter, we describe the background to, and story of, the 'Stories on our Street' project over the past decade, setting out the process and the experience of the authors on the ground as facilitators and participants. We go on to raise a number of questions pertinent to living in post-colonial cities and suggest some responses:

- How do people of goodwill organise for cities based on multiplicity of identities, languages, religions and shared public space?
- What role do theologians and theorists have in fostering collaborative space for faith communities to coexist that work for justice for all people?
- How do our religions and our theologians need to change to foster people of multiple faiths living side by side after empire?
- What role do communities have in organising for cities based on multiplicity of identities?
- In addition, how do we live with the human and other-than-human species with whom we share this planet?

This chapter will tell you about our efforts to build community in a deprived part of Manchester, England. In particular, we document how our neighbours live together, how we created this project and share some of the learning.

On our street, we belong to different spiritual backgrounds: the New Apostolic Church, which has played an active role in this story; Islam, with the Central Manchester Mosque only a few streets away; members of three different Anglican Churches, each with their own blend of Anglicanism from high to low; Catholics, Quakers, Jews, Sikhs and people of no active faith are all present.

We look at some of the neighbourhood activities developed and draw on the stories of the current residents through their own words. We

---

[2] More on the history of the area is held in the Rusholme and Victoria Park Archive.

explore the development of the project out of this sea of community activity.

We reflect on the value of neighbourhood activities alongside local democratic structures. We argue that both are needed to create and underpin the potential for actually living together successfully across different faiths.

Origins of the 'Stories on Our Street' Project

In the summer of 2013, Phil and Helena had the idea of photographing all the residents of the street standing in front of their houses. This idea was not totally new as Elaine had started taking photographs of neighbours at the community street party celebrating the street's 100th birthday in 2011, a few years earlier, but had never finished the task. Their idea, however, was not limited to making a photographic record of those living on Tree Grove now; they also suggested interviewing the residents of each household asking them for similar information to that contained in the 1911 Census and to tell the story of how they came to live here. The idea would be to publish the photographs and stories in a book. This would provide more than a snapshot and record of who was living here in the second decade of the twenty-first century; it would also be a history of typical inner-city Manchester life at this time. It would cover mobility and the effects of world events on ordinary people and the effects of government policies (both international, national and local) on contemporary people. This ambitious project sounded as though it could be a difficult task in practice. Would residents open up? Would it promote cohesion and communal spirit or reveal tensions and difficulties?

The seeds of this project were planted in 2008 with a personal commitment from Phil and Helena to try to make our street a community which worked together for not only its own common good and the good of the street, but also for the longer term goal—the good of the planet.

Tree Grove, an Edwardian residential cul-de-sac located two and a half miles (four kilometres) south of the city centre, was built in the first decade of the twentieth century. For many years, it has been a street of great diversity: diversity in terms of nationalities, religion, age, social class and occupation. At one point in the 1980s, Elaine counted people from 21 different countries and from at least nine different religious traditions living on the street, and it is similar today. Along with this diversity and despite some challenges, it was a friendly street, where many people chatted with each other, helped each other out, got along with each other and respected one another. But it was also a street with significant turn-over of occupancy, some properties run down and poorly managed and crime issues in the neighbourhood. Residents had never worked together for any common aim or shared ideas and not everyone knew each other, particularly now that it seemed that nearly all the adult household was out at work during the day.

In late 2008, Helena applied for and was awarded a grant by Manchester City Council to plant trees on Tree Grove. Whilst they were both working (Helena as a local authority manager of community services and Phil as chief executive of a national environmental charity), Elaine, recently retired from teaching and back in Manchester after a sabbatical, was think-ing about what she wanted to do next. When Phil and Helena knocked on Elaine's door to see if she wanted a street tree planted in front of her house, she was delighted and agreed immediately: "*Yes! I'm very excited about the possibility of street trees on Tree Grove. I loved it when we first moved here and I could shuffle through the autumn leaves and enjoy the dappled summer light. It is sad that they're dying out now or being chopped down for car parking space.*" She also told them that now she was retired she had time to help them with their various projects (they had also just started to organise neighbourhood litter picks from time to time), as she wanted to be involved in something meaningful. At one of the early litter picks—which still take place several times a year, attracting from ten to thirty resi-dents of all ages and faiths and always followed by refreshments—it became obvious that there were people living on Dalton Road, the newly built Estate backing onto Tree Grove who wanted to be connected to the community.

As the authors worked outside in the streets and chatted to neighbours, it quickly became clear that there were several problems that it would be good to sort out. The most pressing was gating the alley between Dalton Road and Tree Grove, to combat theft, drug dealing and prostitution, all of which occurred from time to time in that space. Working together with a growing group of neighbours, this was accomplished. In the process, the Dalton Road and Tree Grove Residents' Association was set up, open to all residents, encouraged by Rusholme Councillors and council officers, formally adopting a Constitution in November 2009. The nascent Residents' Association had held a street party in the spring of 2009 which was a huge success with the neighbours: our street was closed; a fire engine and police car arrived for the children to explore; children's games were organised and food from several cultures was prepared and served by residents. People went around smiling for days. This gave real impetus to the formation of the residents' group and, as a result, these parties remain a popular fixture in the local calendar to this day.

The following year was the 100th anniversary of the first residents moving into houses on Tree Grove and the street party became a birthday party. Harry, one of our neighbours, found a copy of the 1911 census and photocopied it for everyone on the street. Now we all knew who had lived in our houses 100 years ago.[3] At that time, the majority of people came from the north of England; most had live-in servants and many families included children. That is when Elaine first started taking photographs of families; although she only captured a few households ... but it was the germination of what became the 'Stories on our Street' project as we decided to call it.

The authors envisaged that this project would be not only an opportunity to document the street in its present incarnation historically, and to compare it with the street 100 years ago from a census point of view, but that it would also be a tool for furthering the development of our community. As neighbours shared their stories and listened to each other, they would find out how much they had in common and feel valued. People were asked whether they thought the project was a good idea. Everyone said 'Yes,' and the Residents' Association gave it their support. The first interview was conducted in November 2013 and the vast majority were completed within two years. At the time of writing, Elaine and Phil are just finishing up, trying to secure interviews and portraits from the last two or three occupied households (of the 45 on the street built a hundred years ago), and tying up loose ends.

As an interim project, we worked with Jackie Ould-Okojie, the director of the Ahmed Iqbal Ullah Race Relations Resource Centre at Manchester Central Library. She arranged for us to hold a launch at the Library in March 2015. We invited all the neighbours, asked a few of them to tell their stories and gave people an opportunity to view a digital display of photographs along with short summaries of our interviews (including census type information comparable to that collected in 1911).[4] The display is still located in the local history/community area of Central Library on

---

[3] The 1911 Census can be accessed at: https://ukcensusonline.com/search.

[4] For information on visiting the display see: http://www.archivesplus.org/about-archives. Accessed 8 July 2018.

St. Peter's Square, next to Manchester Town Hall. The evening was a
huge success. More than 80 neighbours and friends attended, and we had
to be thrown out by security when the Library closed! People loved telling
their stories and everyone loved listening to them. What we found out was
fascinating, and an insight into our vibrant and multi-layered neighbourhood and the huge variety of early life experiences of our neighbours.
Everyone went away buzzing! It was clear that the publication of these
stories would help bring people together.

The Residents' Association continues to work to improve the feeling of
community both here and on a larger scale. We are trying to make our
community a wildlife corridor, carbon friendly and litter free, and to
increase happiness and connectivity with each other. Our neighbours,
including The New Apostolic Church where we regularly hold our meetings, our local councillors and the Police Community Support Officers
remain committed, and it is clear that the 'Stories on our Street' project
has had a profound impact on the way people see their street and their
neighbours.

One of the amazing things we found out in the course of our interviews
is how many skilled and talented people there are on Tree Grove. Two
teacher/artists, Helen and Nicky, joined us to create *The World on Our
Doorstep* which was published in the autumn of 2017 by the Ahmed Iqbal
Ullah Education Trust and was circulated to all the primary schools in
Manchester.[5] This book is focused on eight diverse households and
includes short biographical information about each family member, draw-
ings by Helen based on Phil's photographs and her research on Edwardian
costume and other information as well as curriculum activities devised by
Nicky. The stories have been adapted to make them suitable for primary
level school children in Manchester aged between eight and eleven, and
not only give children a snapshot of Manchester now compared to a century ago but also give them an insight into how and why so many people
from all around the world have made Manchester their home—a real life
opportunity to see that people of diverse backgrounds have a lot in common and can live together harmoniously.

---

[5] The publication is available to purchase through the Ahmed Iqbal Ullah Resource Centre.

'Stories on Our Street' Project: Methods and Findings

When Phil and Elaine started the project in 2013, we had no idea how it would go. We began with a number of neighbours we knew well to trial our approach, and settled on setting up the interviews in each family's house. Unless circumstances prevented it, we have jointly interviewed the adults in the house and, if they were there and wanted it, any young people. In the case of houses in multiple occupation, we were generally only able to get some of the stories down.

For each interview, we started by explaining what we were doing and why, that we would both be taking handwritten notes and, after the first few, showed examples of what we intended. We made clear that they would have final editorial control and that we would not include anything with which they felt uncomfortable. In the event, very few have done more than make minor factual corrections.

First, we asked for the basic information reported in the 1911 Census—full names, date and place of birth and occupation of all residents. We would then ask each adult to take us through their story, from the circumstances of their birth and their journey through life until they met the other occupants of the house. We would repeat this for each adult present who wished to do so. In some cases, a single adult spoke for the whole household. Once we got to the point in their stories where they met, we asked them about their life together, how it was that they came to live in Tree Grove, and what they thought about living on the street. That is as structured as the interviews were. We would alternate questions and follow up between us as seemed appropriate.

Wherever possible, Phil took a portrait of as many of the household as could be mustered on the day in front of the house, but in many cases the portraits were taken separately. Afterwards, one of us would write up the story from their notes and the other would cross-reference it from theirs. We then provided the interviewees with the text and asked them to approve it.

We have listened to and helped neighbours to share some fascinating stories and have been honoured at the honesty and trust that interviewees have displayed.

Tree Grove was built between 1904 and 1911 and consists of 44 semi-detached and one detached four-bedroom houses. It is a cul-de-sac with a further nine smaller semi-detached houses built during the 1950s. One house was demolished in 1999 to rebuild the New Apostolic Church.

The following information is drawn from our interviews carried out between November 2013 and July 2016. The figures for each house is as reported on the day of its respective interview (Tables 2.1, 2.2, 2.3, and 2.4; Figs. 2.1 and 2.2):

Some typical responses given by interviewees to the question '*How do you feel about living in Tree Grove?*' are set out in the box below. No responses were wholly negative, but a number did refer to issues relating to crime (drugs, burglary, a mugging) as downsides to the area.

> "We were warned against living in Rusholme but we ignored the warnings because we liked the house and location. Now that we are here we like the street, and that it is so international. We are very happy there is a Residents' Association that is caring about the community."
>
> "Even if I won £10 million in the lottery I wouldn't leave this house."
>
> "We were made to feel extremely welcome from the first day."
>
> "When we met the neighbours we knew we had made the right choice."
>
> "If the chips are down there are neighbours who would look out for you. People are friendly. There is a concern on the street for each other. We like the multiculturalism, too."

Table 2.1 Occupancy categories on Tree Grove (collected 2013–2016)

Occupancy	
In multiple occupancy	6
Family	33
Vacant	4
Church	1

Table 2.2 Size of household numbers in Tree Grove (collected 2013–2016)

Household size							
Household size	1	2	3	4	5	6	7
Number of houses	5	8	6	6	5	1	6

Table 2.3 Country of birth of adult residents of Tree Grove (collected 2013–2016)

Place of birth of adult residents							
	England	Wales	Pakistan	Germany	Bangladesh	India	Ireland	Spain
Adults	49	1	9	5	4	3	3	2
	Canada	USA	Romania	France	Somalia	South Africa	Iran	China
Adults	1	1	1	1	1	1	1	1

Table 2.4 Country of birth of children living in Tree Grove (collected 2013–2016)

Country of birth of children	
No of children born in:	
UK	47
Elsewhere	1

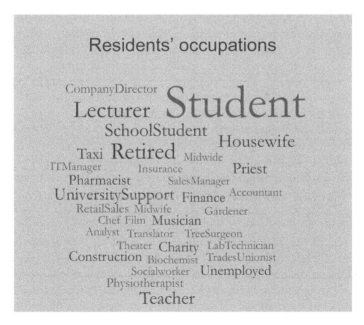

Fig. 2.1 Occupations given by Tree Grove residents (collected 2013–2016). Range 1–20 responses

Fig. 2.2 Reasons given by residents for coming to live on Tree Grove (collected 2013–2016)

Reason given for coming to live in the UK

- Marriage/relationship
- Followed a relative or family
- To look for or take up a job
- One of the Manchester universities or particular course/research offered
  - Several following Erasmus (EU) or other exchanges
- Better school education
- Political turbulence in country of origin
- Visited and stayed

Reflections on the Methodology

So why did the 'Stories on our Street' project work? What were the lessons for its success? There were a number of important elements to the success of the project which included:

- The street has had a relatively stable core; during the two and a half years of the project 11 houses changed occupation—25% of the total. The remaining households have a strong commitment to the area with many of them having lived here for decades.
- Neighbours are clearly delighted with the community activities, improvements and the establishment of the Residents' Association over the five years since we started the project.
- Elaine and Phil were seen to be centrally involved in the Association and the work it has done. Neighbours were generally well disposed towards us, trusted us and wanted to take part!
- We gave interviewees editorial control and stuck to this, and have responded to concerns raised by them.
- We adopted a general format for the interviews, but were relaxed about how they went, following the narrative and interests of the interviewee and the emphasis they adopted in their story; the only 'core' elements were the 1911 census details for current residents.
- During the project, we realised that there were real issues of invasion of privacy and identity theft. Our solution has been to leave out full dates of birth and all surnames (family names). This full information will be lodged with Central Library with a 25-year embargo so that future historians will have access.

- Many neighbours enjoyed telling their story and were keen that it was better known; others were keen to help strengthen cohesion and social capital on our street; a few were more reluctant.

Our challenge now is to find funding to share these journeys, both to inspire other neighbourhoods in south Manchester to do the same, and to disseminate a case study of community cohesion, local heritage and cele-bration of multi-culturalism. Unexpectedly, the Heritage Lottery Fund were not prepared to fund the writing up and presentation of these stories of multi-cultural living history and the dissemination of them into schools, libraries and communities in the wider south Manchester area.[6] As reported above, however, *The World on our Doorstep* has been published and **The History Press** has recently published *Stories of a Manchester Street* to bring to an end a frustrating hiatus in completing the project (Barton and Bishop, 2019).

THE 'STORIES ON OUR STREET' PROJECT IN CONTEXT

We would now like to weave together a number of theoretical threads, which we visualise as brightly coloured strands, reflecting the colours and life to be found in our community. We argue that for communities to thrive, we need a combination of different elements which we hope to illustrate below. Such support calls for a response both from different faith communities, from theologians and government.

Before focusing on our particular street, we would like to draw attention to our context, the radical history of the North West of England. Within only a few miles radius there is the story of the Peterloo Massacre in 1819; the founding of the co-operative movement in Rochdale in 1844; the Pankhurst Centre where Emily Pankhurst worked for votes for women; the meeting of the Fifth Pan-African Congress in 1945 at the former Chorlton on Medlock Town Hall just down the road, with delegates such as Kwame Nkrumah and Jomo Kenyatta; the radical Asian Youth Movement of the 1970s and 1980s; an early meeting of the movement for LGBT equality in the offices of the Diocese of Manchester and the pioneering Gay Village and "It's Queer Up North" Festival established in the 1980s.[7]

---

[6] See https://www.hlf.org.uk/looking-funding/our-grant-programmes/sharing-heritage for more details.

[7] For details of the radical history of Greater Manchester, see the People's History Museum, which has an online collection at: http://www.phm.org.uk/ and the WCLM: the Working

The first thread we'd like to explore relates to the community activities described above. A wide range of theoretical inputs such as the UK government's *National Strategy for Neighbourhood Renewal,* the *Community Development Challenge* report, and scholars Alison Gilchrist and Marilyn Taylor's work on defining and outlining the work of community development have been published since the millennium.[8] All argue that local communities need support to grow together, including financial expertise, grants, community spaces/buildings and community support workers with community development training and expertise. Community development has strong values and ethics and also is about learning and empowering all members of the community.[9] Without such support, we would argue, communities of multiple identities will find it challenging to grow together. In diverse areas such as Rusholme, which benefit from pockets of strong social capital, communities can do it themselves for a period of time. However, analysis shows that strong sustainable input is needed.[10] For example, if a group is to apply for grants they need a constitution, a committee, a treasurer, to know how to fill in the application form and provide monitoring data. Frequently these skills need to be coupled with an ability to understand the 'code' and jargon of the funder; from 'strategy' to 'outcome' from 'diversity' to 'impact.'

For some of the challenges we have faced in our neighbourhood, we needed a resilient committee, for example, in the face of the need to tackle the persistent rubbish and litter, and of private landlords who do not care about the community. The Committee has benefited from consistent support and trusted relationships with our democratically elected local

---

Class History Movement Library at: http://www.wcml.org.uk/. For the Asian Youth Movement, see Anandi Ramamurthy, *Britain's Asian Youth Movement* (London: Pluto Press, 2013).

[8] Cabinet Office Social Exclusion Unit, *A New Commitment to Neighbourhood Renewal: National Strategy Action Plan* (London: Crown, 2001) http://www.bris.ac.uk/poverty/downloads/keyofficialdocuments/Neighbourhood%20Renewal%20National%20Strategy%20Report.pdf. Accessed 8 July 2018.

Communities and Local Government (CLG), *The Community Development Challenge Report* (London: Crown, 2006) http://webarchive.nationalarchives.gov.uk/20120920061419/http://www.communities.gov.uk/documents/communities/pdf/153241.pdf.

Alison Gilchrist and Marilyn Taylor, *The Short Guide to Community Development* (Bristol: Bristol University Press, 2011).

[9] CLG, *The Community Development Challenge Report.*

[10] Robert Putnam, *Bowling Alone – The Collapse and Revival of American Community* (New York: Simon and Schuster, 2000).

councillors who have frequently encouraged us and supported us by 'unblocking' an issue within the council bureaucracy and securing small grants for our activities.

There is extensive evidence of the effectiveness in building and sustaining strong inter-faith communities through interventions such as neighbourhood wardens, community development workers and outreach from local hubs—schools, community buildings and doctors' surgeries, for example. After many years, we know how to do it in the UK; we have the research showing how to grow communities, such as from the Joseph Rowntree Foundation and past governments.[11]

But in the "Age of Austerity" initiated in the UK by the crash of 2008—the year we started our work on Tree Grove—community support has not been the policy of this government in the UK. Nearly all the funding for community development has gone. This is arguably a key factor in the alienation and dissatisfaction amongst 'left behind' communities which resulted in the narrow vote for Brexit in June 2016 as evidenced through research for the Joseph Rowntree Foundation.[12]

The second thread is Anne Primavesi's concept of 'Gift Exchange.' Primavesi argues that gift exchanges are not a commodity and are not monetarised, in contrast to the neo-liberal western dominant paradigm

---

[11] See Marilyn Taylor, Mandy Wilson, Derrick Purdue, and Pete Wilde, *Changing Neighbourhoods: The Impact of Light Touch Community Development Support in 20 Communities* (York: Joseph Rowntree Foundation, 2007) https://www.jrf.org.uk/report/changing-neighbourhoods-impact-light-touch-support-20-communitiesreports.

Office of the Deputy Prime Minister (ODPM), Neighbourhood Renewal Unit, *New Deal for Communities, the National Evaluation Annual Report, 2003/2004* (London: Crown, 2004).

ODPM, Social Exclusion Unit, *Breaking the Cycle, Taking Stock of Progress and Priorities for the Future, Social Exclusion Unit Report*, Summary (London: Crown, 2004).

ODPM, Social Exclusion Unit, *Neighbourhood Management Pathfinder Programme National Evaluation*, Annual Review 2003/4 & Key Findings (London: Crown, 2004).

Communities and Local Government (CLG) 'Learning to Change Neighbourhoods, Lessons from the Guide Neighbourhoods Programme,' Summary Evaluation Report (London: Crown, 2007).

CLG, *Place Making* (London: Crown, 2008).

CLG, 'Evaluation of the National Strategy for Neighbourhood Renewal: Local Research Project, Executive Summary,' ECOTEC Research and Consulting Ltd. (London: Crown, 2010).

[12] Goodwin, Matthew and Heath Oliver (2016) "The Brexit Vote Explained: Poverty, Low Skills and Lack of Opportunities," York: Joseph Rowntree Foundation. https://www.jrf.org.uk/report/brexit-vote-explained-poverty-low-skills-and-lack-opportunities.

which monetarises all exchanges as a matter of course.[13] When we pick up rubbish from the streets we are not asking for a monetary return, but the relationships established through this process of gift exchange might, as happened in our community, create a women's book club and a knitting group. When we meet together, we create neighbourhood days and street parties, and we also think about the homeless. Anne Primavesi also puts the idea of gift exchanges in the context of the environment and all the gifts we get from the planet so freely such as water, sunshine and air to breathe.[14]

This leads to our third thread; growing identity beyond the simply human. Our multiple identity includes the fellow species we share the world with—the trees and the bees are integral part of our communities—but we rarely acknowledge it in our daily lives. Elaine has been co-ordinating a 'Bee Day,' when we seek to help bees on our street through the planting of appropriate flowers. Two of our neighbours, Nicky and Phil, help people who do not feel skilled in this area to garden. All the faith communities Phil and Helena have researched have a strong notion of stewardship and our responsibility to take care of the planet and of our fellow species that face such human induced devastation.[15]

The fourth thread arising from our work is one of power. We can take Steven Lukes' analysis of the different faces of power and consider the different ways we experience and exercise different forms of power in our neighbourhood.[16] Powerful corporations, for example, take minimal responsibility for the impacts, for good or bad, of their operations in the community. Bellway imposed a new estate into the physical, arboricultural and social matrix of Victoria Park, sold it, and moved on. Tesco has opened three stores almost equidistant from our street in the past decade, with no concern for their impact on the local retail economy, or for social capital generated by independently owned micro-businesses such as shopkeepers, or for the traffic they generate. Central government too exerts major power on our community from decisions to close our Post Office on Rusholme's High Street, to weaken the protection of tenants from unscrupulous landlords and, of course, the decision to withdraw huge sums of

[13] Anne Primavesi, *Gaia's Gift: Earth, Ourselves and God after Copernicus* (London: Routledge, 2003) 116.

[14] Anne Primavesi, *Gaia and Climate Change, A Theology of Gift Events* (London: Routledge, 2009) 88.

[15] The Forum for Religion and Ecology at Yale University gives official statements on Religion and Ecology from a wide variety of faith communities.

[16] Steven Lukes, *Power: A Radical View, the Original Text with Two Major New Chapters*, 2nd edition (London: Palgrave Macmillan, 1974 & 2005).

financial support to Manchester City Council, leading indirectly to adverse consequences including homeless people forced onto the streets, an avalanche of rubbish which the council is unable to keep up with, and the dilution of the system of neighbourhood managers and integration of local services. The City Council too, although constrained by national frameworks, is powerful locally, through its decisions on traffic management, parking, waste disposal contracts, planning policies and licensing of private landlords. We are also unconsciously influenced by the power of advertisers and the media, with Rusholme portrayed as being a dangerous and rundown neighbourhood, with an undue focus on the Curry Mile.

There are different political responses on our street and different analyses of power. The response as members of a community has been to say that individual power is important, alongside collective power working together with our neighbours to change the world. Therefore, we take for inspiration the quote from the monk Thomas Merton:

> *Living is more than submission; it is creation.*
> *We can begin now to change this street and this city.*
> *We will begin to discover our power to transform the world.*[17]

We have tried to take on the positive aspects of power, of working with each other to create a better world, but recognising that our collective empowerment has its limits as a result of externally powerful sources and the limits to our ability to formulate locally universal positions on some key issues. Despite these limitations, as this case study demonstrates, real progress is possible through an appreciative lens.[18]

Our **final thread** is the role faith communities and academics can play in facilitating people of multiple identifies living together. Our experience leads us to believe that faith communities have a key outreach role beyond their own members, and that this needs to be argued mosque by church, temple by chapel. On our street, our residents' group would not have grown without the free use of the kitchen and meeting room provided by a local church. In a gift exchange, Phil collected £2 coins in his change and

---

[17] Thomas Merton, quoted in B. Browne, 'Imagine Chicago: A Methodology for Cultivating Community,' *Journal of Community & Applied Social Psychology* (14, 2004) 394–405.

[18] Appreciative inquiry suggests drawing on the best in people and communities to dream and achieve hopeful futures: https://appreciativeinquiry.champlain.edu/learn/appreciative-inquiry-introduction/.

gave the money to Dennis, warden of the church, who has spent it on funding solar powered lights in his village in Zambia, reducing the use of dangerous kerosene lamps.

How can this role of faith communities be debated and grown when many faith communities find it a challenge to simply keep their own work going within their congregation? It is a fact that they all have an infrastructure, are located out in communities, have similar core values in terms of humanity, relief of poverty and environmental stewardship, and could potentially be more effective if they worked better together.[19]

What, then, of the academic community and theologians? We would argue that universities have an important role in researching, voicing and explaining how people of different faiths can successfully live together by making manifest the support needs of neighbourhoods, the issues of power that individuals and communities need to work with and the evidence of successful community development outcomes. Such a role is not, however, confined to the walls of academia and within academic journals. It needs to go beyond the exercise of research ratings assessments. And it needs to actively engage with students, government, business, non-governmental organisations (NGOs), faith groups and communities where they are located beyond the academic institution.[20]

So how might this be achieved? Helena's first job was at the University of Manchester's Students' Union, where she was recruited to link the University to the (deprived) community of Hulme in inner Manchester adjacent to the main campus in the late 1970s. She soon discovered, however, that her role was expected to facilitate students undertaking work in the community, in itself a laudable aim, but was **not** about the university staff working with the community and applying their expertise to real life neighbourhood challenges. Years later, in the mid-1990s, Phil took a role designed to facilitate academic engagement in real life environmental issues affecting small businesses and found much the same reluctance for the vast majority of academics to engage.

[19] See Adam Dinham, "What Is a 'Faith Community'" *Community Development Journal* 46 (4, 2010) 526–54. See also resources on the Faith-based Regeneration Network: http://www.fbrn.org.uk/about-fbrn.

[20] Marilyn Mayo, Zoraida Mediwelso-Bendek, Carol Packham (eds.) *Community Research for Community Development* (London: Palgrave, 2013).

Susanne Martikke, Andrew Church, and Angie Heart, *Greater than the Sum of Its Parts: What Works in Sustaining Community-University Partnerships* (Manchester: GMCVO, 2015) https://www.gmcvo.org.uk/greater-sum-its-parts-what-works-sustaining-community-university-partnerships (accessed 9 March 2017).

One way to address this issue in terms of how academics work would be to develop the field of participatory action research and its crucial perspective, as argued by Reason and Bradbury, that the researcher and the subjects of the research are, in fact, co-researchers and not subject and object.[21] The empowerment of those co-researchers was explored by Bradbury and Reason as they developed their notions of an emerging participatory paradigm and point to a radically new way for academics and academic institutions to work with communities to mutual benefit.[22] Rusholme has many challenges. We have more than 70,000 students from all over the world only one or two miles away and over 16,000 staff employed in two major universities.[23] Were universities and communities to work more closely together, we could address problems and grow a greener, more resilient and sustainable Rusholme. How universities could develop through teaching and research to respond to the needs of their local communities as community anchors and hubs is explored through Goddard et al.[24]

SOME FINAL CONCLUSIONS

In terms of our spirituality, the authors all come from different faith traditions, but we all respect and value all faiths as well as people of goodwill with no faith. Spirit and Love are manifest in many ways. We have tried to live this in practice in our community, for example, through the annual decorating of our street trees on the 24 December, centred on children, which includes chocolates, laughter, baubles and tinsel. Similarly, we gathered to celebrate and honour the life and death of Nelson Mandela in our community garden and people from different origins and identities were able to voice their shared appreciation of his life. And when we held a small street market in the grounds of the New Apostolic Church to raise funds to support those caught up in major flooding in Pakistan. And again

---

[21] Peter Reason and Hilary Bradbury 'Preface' in Peter Reason and Hilary Bradbury (eds.) *Handbook of Action Research Concise* (paperback edition) (London: Sage, 2006) i–xxxi.

[22] Peter Reason, and Hilary Bradbury 'Introduction: Inquiry and Participation in Search of World Worthy of Human Aspiration' in Peter Reason and Hilary Bradbury (eds.) *Handbook of Action Research Concise* (paperback edition) (London: Sage, 2006) 1–14.

[23] For further details on the two universities, see: https://www.manchester.ac.uk/discover/facts-figures/ and https://www2.mmu.ac.uk/media/mmuacuk/content/documents/about/corporate-strategy/Manchester-Met-Corporate-Brochure-A6.pdf.

[24] John Goddard, Ellen Hazelkorn, Louise Kempton, and Paul Vallence (eds.) *The Civic University, the Policy and Leadership Challenges* (Cheltenham: Edward Elgar, 2016).

last year when we planted a Yorkshire Rose in our community garden to honour the work and memory of British MP Jo Cox, and just recently (May 2018) with the pastor, local councillors and residents, we dedicated a yew sapling to the memory of our deceased MP of 47 years, Sir Gerald Kaufman, in the grounds of the New Apostolic Church. We believe that such interventions create Spirit in a new form. Over time, a notion of faithfulness and of renewed and willing gift exchange is needed to keep doing the work in community; to keep on doing it and to ensure that we freely empower others so that the important work of building community is kept going when we personally are not there to do it.

Thomas Berry learnt from working with both eastern and western religious traditions and argued that the universe is an interconnected whole from the Big Bang to the furthermost galaxy, and that we are all part of this interconnected whole.[25] When we grow community and weave together people of multiple identities to live together harmoniously, we are building humanity back into the deep structures of the universe.

Acknowledgements Grateful thanks to the members of the Residents Association, for their time, participation, support and faith in the Project; to Helen Glaizner, Nicky Johnson and Harry Spooner; our local Councillors, Rabnawaz Akbar, Ahmed Ali and Jill Lovecy; the New Apostolic Church and Jackie Ould-Okojie; and Elizabeth Parish for their encouragement and support.

BIBLIOGRAPHY

Ahmed Iqbal Ullah Race Relations Resource Centre. http://www.racearchive.manchester.ac.uk/. Accessed 30 January 2017.

Barton, P., and E. Bishop. 2019. *Stories of a Manchester Street*. Stroud: History Press.

Barton, P., E. Bishop, N. Johnson, and H. Glaizner. 2017. *The World on Our Doorstep: An Educational Activity Book for 8–12 Year Olds*. Manchester: Ahmed Iqbal Ullah Race Relations Resource Centre.

Berry, Thomas. 1988. *The Dream of the Earth*. San Francisco: Sierra Club.

———. 1999. *The Great Work, Our Way into the Future*. New York: Bell Tower.

Cabinet Office Social Exclusion Unit. 2001. *A New Commitment to Neighbourhood Renewal: National Strategy Action Plan*. London: Crown. http://www.bris.

[25] Thomas Berry, *The Dream of the Earth* (San Francisco: Sierra Club, 1988).
Thomas Berry, *The Great Work, Our Way into the Future* (New York, NY: Bell Tower, 1999).

ac.uk/poverty/downloads/keyofficialdocuments/Neighbourhood%20 Renewal%20National%20Strategy%20Report.pdf. Accessed 8 July 2018.

Census 1911. https://ukcensusonline.com/search. Accessed 8 July 2018.

Communities and Local Government (CLG). 2006. *The Community Development Challenge Report*. London: Crown. http://webarchive.nationalarchives.gov. uk/20120920061419/http://www.communities.gov.uk/documents/communities/pdf/153241.pdf.

———. 2007. *Learning to change neighbourhoods, Lessons from the Guide Neighbourhoods Programme*. Summary Evaluation Report. London: Crown.

———. 2008. *Place Making*. London: Crown.

———. 2010. *Evaluation of the National Strategy for Neighbourhood Renewal: Local Research Project, Executive Summary*. ECOTEC Research and Consulting Ltd.

Dinham, Adam. 2010. What Is a 'Faith Community'. *Community Development Journal* 46 (4): 526–554.

Forum for Religion and Ecology. *Official Statements on Religion and Ecology*. http://fore.yale.edu/publications/statements. Accessed 9 July 2018.

Gilchrist, Alison, and Marilyn Taylor. 2011. *The Short Guide to Community Development*. Bristol: Bristol University Press.

Goddard, John, Ellen Hazelkorn, Louise Kempton, and Paul Vallence, eds. 2016. *The Civic University, the Policy and Leadership Challenges*. Cheltenham: Edward Elgar.

Goodwin, Matthew, and Heath Oliver. 2016. *The Brexit Vote Explained: Poverty, Low Skills and Lack of Opportunities*. York: Joseph Rowntree Foundation. https://www.jrf.org.uk/report/brexit-vote-explained-poverty-low-skills-and-lack-opportunities.

Joseph Rowntree Foundation: Taylor, Marilyn, Mandy Wilson, Purdue Derrick, and Wilde Pete. 2007. *Changing Neighbourhoods: The Impact of Light Touch Community Development Support in 20 Communities*. https://www.jrf.org. uk/report/changing-neighbourhoods-impact-light-touch-support-20-communities.

Lukes, Steven. 1974 & 2005. *Power: A Radical View, the Original Text with Two Major New Chapters*. 2nd ed. London: Palgrave Macmillan.

Manchester City Council, *Indices of Deprivation 2015. A Briefing Note on Manchester's Relative Levels of Deprivation Using Measures Produced by DCLG, Including the Index of Multiple Deprivation*, (2015).

Martikke, Susanne, Andrew Church, and Angie Heart. 2015. *Greater Than the Sum of Its Parts: What Works in Sustaining Community-University Partnerships*. Manchester: GMCVO. https://www.gmcvo.org.uk/greater-sum-its-parts-what-works-sustaining-community-university-partnerships. Accessed 9 March 2017.

Mayo, Marilyn, Zoraida Mediwelso-Bendek, and Carol Packham, eds. 2013. *Community Research for Community Development*. London: Palgrave.

Merton, Thomas. 2004. Quoted in B. Browne. Imagine Chicago: A Methodology for Cultivating Community. *Journal of Community & Applied Social Psychology* 14: 394–405.

ODPM (Office of the Deputy Prime Minister), Neighbourhood Renewal Unit. 2004. *New Deal for Communities, the National Evaluation Annual Report, 2003/2004*. London: Crown.

ODPM (Office of the Deputy Prime Minister), Social Exclusion Unit. 2004a. *Breaking the Cycle, Taking Stock of Progress and Priorities for the Future, Social Exclusion Unit Report, Summary*. London: Crown.

———. 2004b. *Neighbourhood Management Pathfinder Programme National Evaluation, Annual Review 2003/4 & Key Findings*. London: Crown.

Primavesi, Anne. 2003. *Gaia's Gift: Earth, Ourselves and God After Copernicus*. London: Routledge.

———. 2009. *Gaia and Climate Change, A Theology of Gift Events*. London: Routledge.

Putnam, Robert. 2000. *Bowling Alone – The Collapse and Revival of American Community*. New York: Simon and Schuster.

Ramamurthy, Anandi. 2013. *Britain's Asian Youth Movement*. London: Pluto Press.

Reason, Peter, and Hilary Bradbury. 2006. Introduction: Inquiry and Participation in Search of World Worthy of Human Aspiration. In *Handbook of Action Research Concise*, ed. Peter Reason and Hilary Bradbury, Paperback ed., 1–14. London: Sage.

Reason, Peter, and Bradbury Hilary. 2006. Preface. In *Handbook of Action Research Concise*, ed. Peter Reason and Hilary Bradbury, Paperback ed., i–xxxi. London: Sage.

Rusholme and Victoria Park Archive. http://rusholmearchive.org. Accessed 4 April 2016.

CHAPTER 3

Multifaith Space: Religious Accommodation in Postcolonial Public Space?

Terry Biddington

Religious Pluralism in South Asia

While the history of Western Christendom has witnessed religious pluralism only exceptionally—most notoriously in those periods where the presence of Jews was tolerated solely for reasons of financial and political
expediency—the religious history of South Asia may, with some accuracy,
be described as one of religiously plural cohabitation going back centuries.

Both Yoginder Sikand and Afsar Mohammad have, for instance, docu-
mented the long history of overlapping and shared religious spaces and
practices that exist at a popular level in many parts of India.[1] Mohammad,
in particular, offers a fascinating account of what he terms "the emergence
of a shared devotional space" in his close analysis of one not-untypical

---

[1] Yoginder Sikand, *Sacred Spaces: Exploring Traditions of Shared Faith in India* (New
Delhi: Penguin Books India, 2003). Afsar Mohammad, *The Festival of Pirs: Popular Islam
and Shared Devotion in South India* (Oxford: Oxford University Press, 2013).

T. Biddington (✉)
University of Winchester, Winchester, UK
e-mail: Terry.Biddington@winchester.ac.uk

© The Author(s) 2019   35
J. Dunn et al. (eds.), *Multiple Faiths in Postcolonial
Cities*, Postcolonialism and Religions,
https://doi.org/10.1007/978-3-030-17144-5_3

example, the small village of Gugudu, east of Ananta Puram district, in south India.[2]

Although Gugudu is a majority Hindu village, its Hindu shrine (the Chenna Kesava Swami Temple) is largely ignored, and the mosque for its minority Shi'a Muslim population is poorly attended. The vast majority of the villagers and those from the surrounding area practice a shared devotion to a "pir," or Sufi "saint," who is understood to be the Hindu deity Ram reincarnated with a new avatar as the Sufi Muslim figure Kullayappa.

The "Pir House" at the centre of the villages attracts thousands of Hindus and Muslims from across the region and beyond throughout the year, but especially during the Shi'a festival of Muharram or, as it is known locally, the "Festival of Pirs." Worshippers follow devotions and practices in the Pir House that are clearly a mixture of Hindu and Sufi religious elements (designated by the hybrid term "fateha puja") that are said to go back seven or eight hundred years, and which are described by Mohammad as "a popular manifestation of Islamic devotion ... that, in a pluralistic context keeps itself in a dynamic dialogue with non-Muslim practices."[3] The result is a shared "public devotional space ... that clearly privileges a pluralist form of devotional life," but one that is now being increasingly contested by more mainstream and normative forms of both Hinduism and Shi'a Islam that are attempting to re-assert themselves against these localised and ancient expressions of shared public religiosity.[4]

Sikand, in his own study, makes clear the extent to which these shared religious spaces are both historically widespread and persistent throughout south India and beyond and yet also increasingly contested. He describes with regret how "a hundred darghas [Sufi shrines] or more where Hindus and Muslims [have] for centuries, worshipped together have been reduced to rubble by violent mobs, encouraged by the agencies of the State."[5]

However, despite the recent resurgence everywhere of Hindutva—Hindu nationalism—something of the continued underlying acceptance of the religious pluralism endemic to the subcontinent is still to be seen at the Epiphany Cathedral in Dornakal, in Andhra Pradesh state.[6] Consecrated in 1939 after a design by Bishop Azariah, the first Indian bishop of the

[2] Mohammad, *The Festival of Pirs*, 26.
[3] Ibid., 2.
[4] Ibid., 3–4.
[5] Sikand, *Sacred Spaces*, 270.
[6] See http://www.findmessages.com/tag/epiphany-cathedral. Accessed 19/7/2016.

Church of South India, its intention to be a recognisably Indian religious building is communicated by its use of Islamic architectural features—alongside traditional Christian symbolism—to adorn a layout that mimics the indigenous design of a Hindu temple.

Elsewhere, the Laxmi Narayan Hindu Temple also known as the Birla Temple, in the north Indian state of Jaipur, returns the architectural complement by merging to great effect the familiar tiered Hindu tower, with a Buddhist stupa and Islamic dome.[7] Built as late as 1988, the outside walls of the temple also display carvings of other great world religious leaders: Buddha, Confucius, and Christ—but also Socrates and Zarathustra—seeking to illustrate the essential unity of all religious truth.

Interestingly, however, while such religious pluralism is typical of the south Asian context and should be celebrated as a means of embodying acceptance of religious "otherness" and—for the most part—tolerance, such an open attitude cannot always be assumed when it comes to access to religious spaces (shared or otherwise) for women or those deemed to be of lower caste. For, notwithstanding recent successful high-profile challenges, women's access to sacred space is still problematical in some places.[8] And the exclusion of Dalits that is everywhere commonplace means that in many ways the pressing issue in South Asia is neither religious pluralism nor religiously shared sacred space, but the provision of religious space that is gender- and caste-inclusive.[9]

FURTHER WEST

However, while such traditional and widespread manifestations of the openness of places of worship to religious pluralism appear normative in an Indian context, as we move further West and forward in time the overt presence of multiple religions—as both a sometimes tolerated and often contested public reality—has remained confined to those regions where multiple religions have overlapped historically, such as the Middle East and the Balkans.

[7] See http://www.indialine.com/travel/rajasthan/jaipur/birla-temple.html. Accessed 19/7/2016.

[8] See http://www.dnaindia.com/india/report-shani-temple-sabarimala-sree-padmanabhaswamy-haji-ali-entry-to-women-2196954. Accessed 14/7/2016.

[9] See http://timesofindia.indiatimes.com/india/Tarun-Vijay-Dalits-pelted-with-stone-for-defying-temple-ban/articleshow/52367193.cms. Accessed 14/7/2016.

From the seventh century CE, both the church of the Nativity in Bethlehem and the Byzantine Basilica of Saint John the Baptist in Damascus allowed Muslims to pray in the unadorned "narthex" area at the eastern end of the church.[10] By around the year 1000 CE, St Catherine's monastery in the Sinai desert of Egypt had a mosque and minaret inside the sacred precincts that is still used today by the Bedouin who serve the community. Though, arguably, this arrangement was established more out of a pragmatic desire to protect the monastery from attack, rather than out of concern for the spiritual wellbeing of the Muslim servants. Be that as it may, as late as 1983, the mixed Christian-Muslim Palestinian West Bank town of Beit Sahour contained an ancient underground cistern above which a shrine to the Virgin Mary was built "expressly for the devotional use of both Muslims and Christians of all denominations."[11]

In Macedonia, the Holy Mother of God Most Pure convent in Kicevo continues to keep its narthex free from Christian symbols for the benefit of Muslim pilgrims who come to pray for healing and the conception of children and, in nearby Makedonski Brod, the shrine of St Nicholas hosts Christian and Muslim worship during the December feast of St Nicholas and the spring festival of St George and of his Muslim avatar "Al Khidr." While these worship events occur separately and sequentially, there is, nonetheless, a curious mingling of practices. The Muslims, for instance, pray towards the Orthodox iconostasis rather than towards Mecca and drink the holy water (blessed by the priest) as an "aid to good health" rather than use it for ritual ablutions. (There is no wudu facility.) Both the Christians and the various Muslim groups light candles, distribute red Easter eggs, and venerate the tomb of the unknown saint with equal fervour. And, in recent years, both groups have come under pressure by more orthodox authorities, at home and from abroad, to reject these localised forms of heterodox religiosity in favour of more normatively exclusive forms of practice.

Moving still further into western Europe, the first shared Catholic-Protestant church is thought to be the "Simultankirche" or "inter-denominational" church that was created around 1524 at St Peter's in

---

[10] C. Emmett, "The Siting of Churches and Mosques as an Indicator of Christian-Muslim Relations," *Islam and Christian-Muslim Relations*, 20:4 (2009), 451–476 at 461.

[11] G. Bowman, "Orthodox-Muslim Interactions at 'Mixed Shrines' in Macedonia," in Chris Hann and Hermann Goltz eds. *Eastern Christians in Anthropological Perspective* (California: University of California Press, 2010).

Bautzen, the earliest of many such churches in Germany. The sanctuary was divided by a four-metre (twelve-foot) high screen (since removed) as a pragmatic response to the religious concerns of the inhabitants and, to this day, the original separate Catholic and Protestant entrances, altars, and even organs remain, with public denominational worship taking place at different times.[12]

After the Reformation, such dual churches became common across the German-speaking parts of Europe where there were Catholics and Protestants in equal numbers. And though their origins may lie in the necessity of their religiously turbulent times, they bear witness to a desire for religious tolerance, at least, that was to be manifestly absent in other parts of Europe.

Similar pragmatism also appears to have informed Friedrich Wilhelm I of Prussia who, in 1732, set up an Islamic prayer room in his Potsdam palace for the 20 Turkish mercenaries who were his personal body guards. In so doing, he displayed a radical, if self-interested, degree of concern for the needs of his employees that was to remain unrivalled for centuries to come.

THE TWENTIETH CENTURY

In the US, Boston Logan International Airport created the first multi-denominational chapel in 1951. This was followed in 1955 by a tri-denominational chapel at the Massachusetts Institute of Technology, also in Boston, and at the US Air Force Cadet Academy in Colorado Springs in 1962.

This pragmatic acknowledgement of plural religious needs was mirrored in the development of hospital chapels. The American Hospital Association reported in 1974 that 55% of hospitals had a chapel for multi-denominational use, many of which had been converted from single usage since the 1950s, though further upgrading to multifaith usage typically did not happen until the late 1990s.[13] This development was often paralleled by a shift in activity in these spaces from communal Christian worship to individual silent acts of intercessory prayer or meditation as the

---

[12] http://www.oberlausitz.com/ferien/kulturell/via-sacra/de/dom-st.petri-domschatz-kammer-bautzen.aspx Accessed 23/11/16. In German.

[13] Wendy Cadge, *Paging God: Religion in the Halls of Medicine* (Chicago: University of Chicago Press, 2013), 57.

multi-*religious* identity of the spaces changed into a more individualistic multi*faith* one.

In 1957, Dag Hammarskjöld, Secretary General of the United Nations, created a multifaith "Meditation Room" at its New York headquarters, while a 1960s "quiet space" for non-Christians and atheists was available in William Hulme's Grammar School in Manchester (UK) for several decades. At around the same time, the famous Rothko chapel, in Houston Texas, was opened in 1964 and still offers a space for private celebrations and life events for all faiths and none.[14]

Back in Europe, the first explicitly inclusive new-build Multifaith Space (a "Meditation Space" or "Andachtsraum") was established at Vienna airport in 1988, described as a "place of peace and tranquility in the midst of the busy airport."[15] This pioneer development has been followed by the creation of both purpose-built and retrofitted multifaith spaces (hereafter "MFS"), in a wide variety of contexts: not just airports and hospitals, but prisons, schools and universities, shopping centres and malls, sports stadia, offices and factories, and even motorway service stations and rest-stops.

THE SPREAD OF MFS IN THE WESTERN PUBLIC REALM

Today, there are many thousands of MFS in Europe, the UK and US alone, and growing numbers in South America and the Far East, along with others in countries with active inter-religious tensions.[16] The presence of MFS speaks concretely both about the current importance of the public face of religion on the world stage as well as of its increased visibility in our local communities. Indeed, a recent international research project has demonstrated how MFS are both *symptoms* of the contemporary secular landscape and *agents* of further social and attitudinal change.[17] The interplay between being both agent and symptom of that change can be illustrated with reference to the development of public worship space in a

[14] http://rothkochapel.org/experience/private-services/. Accessed 14/7/16.

[15] http://www.viennaairport.com/en/passengers/airport/prayer_room. Accessed 23/11/16.

[16] For example, the cardiac surgery centre in Khartoum, Sudan. See Robert Klanten & Lukas Feireiss, eds. *Closer to God: Religious Architecture and Sacred Spaces* (Berlin: Gestalten, 2010).

[17] R. Brand, A. Crompton, C. Hewson, T. Biddington, *Multi-Faith Spaces: Symptoms and Agents of Religious and Social Change.* AHRC Religion and Society Programme AH/H017321/1 (2010–2013).

leading, though not-untypical, community National Health Service hospital in the UK.

The first chapel at what is now the Manchester Royal Infirmary was built in 1908 as a mainstream Protestant chapel designed for the communal gathering of patients, families, and hospital staff at a time when public worship was more generally acknowledged as being an integral aid to physical recovery. In the 1980s, this chapel was declared unfit for purpose, not only on account of the evident structural dilapidation of the building but because of the impact of new equality, anti-discrimination, and health and safety legislation, but also because of the demands of the legal requirement for the equitable allocation of healthcare services on the basis of the changing ethnic and cultural diversity of the local demographic served by the hospital.

Consequently, the chapel was replaced by an MFS comprising a suite of small discrete retrofitted rooms for Muslims and Christians and other faith groups (all originally offices and service areas) adjoining a central corridor. Each major faith had its own allocated space within the corridor which became, therefore, the only truly communal or shared religious space. A space that was then required to be as neutral—"non-offensive"—as possible, with only legitimate worship activities and times, rules of use, and health and safety regulations on display alongside the contact details of authorised chaplains and faith advisers. Moreover, the inevitable impingement on this shared space at times of peak demand (particularly for Muslim patients, staff and visitors) and the potential for misunderstanding, offence, and even conflict had to be carefully managed by chaplaincy staff so as to maintain the precarious balance between authentic needs and sometimes incompatible expectations.

The Experience of MFS

The experience of sharing and managing this retrofitted space, alongside the increasing pressures upon its limited capacity caused by the needs of an ever-increasing ethnically large and diverse user base, resulted in the replacement of this suite of rooms in 2008 with a purpose-built MFS, which was not only a response to the then very changed demographic of the Greater Manchester area served by the hospital but also, at the same time, an attempt to anticipate and respond to the current and future needs of the hospital community itself.

Thus, the current attractive oval- (or "womb"-) shaped worship space is divided by a rather attractive moveable wooden screen to create two equally sized spaces. In the adjacent corridors are chaplains' offices, toilet and ablution facilities, and storage for religious artefacts available as required. One of these spaces—with a further internal divider to facilitate traditional gender segregation—is permanently reserved for Muslim prayer and the other—containing an altar and chairs, a small organ, and a "prayer tree"—is available for everyone else for periodic collective (and effectively only ever Christian) worship or, more typically, individual prayer, meditation and silence for members of all the world faiths and none. The reality though—given daily needs and weekly peak time pressures—is that this second space is, by default, an area that might more accurately—if perhaps not uncontroversially—be termed as being for "non-Muslims" and which is typically prioritised for Muslim prayer as necessity dictates.

This new flexible arrangement is managed by the chaplaincy team to ensure equitable needs-based access, a fair and decent ordering of religious paraphernalia in the adjacent corridor, and the maximum respect for and by all users. It works well. However, in MFS where such active—indeed pro-active—management is absent, one group or other will tend, if not always consciously, to recreate the expected conditions of its own faith tradition: be it the use of screens to separate men and women, a table or religious paraphernalia to suggest or even underscore worship of one specific faith, or proselytising literature or publicity to visibly promote one creed or set of faith-based activities over others.

THE "CONTESTED AMBIGUITY" OF MFS IN SECULAR INSTITUTIONS

The creation of this particular hospital MFS—and a phenomenon reflected elsewhere across the spectrum of such spaces in Western public institutions—is the result of a desire for cost-effective pragmatic inclusivity, enshrined in equal opportunities legislation, which seeks to provide a clear and symptomatic response to the diverse needs of the community at large.

Yet what is perhaps noticeably different in this Western multifaith institutional public space—certainly in comparison with the accepted and largely unproblematic normativity of seeing people of other faith at prayer in the south Asian context—is not only the absence of widespread experience of other religious practices, but the still sadly not-untypical occurrence of a problematic "surprised embarrassment," "inner distress," "spiritual conflict," or even "physical revulsion" on the part of some MFS users when worship or prayers in one area is clearly inferred, visible, or audible in another. At such times, mild feelings of embarrassment or even more strongly of offence, as well as fears of actual spiritual or religious "contamination" are sometimes recorded, with the result that some people or groups simply refuse to use shared space.[18]

For although MFS may typically be the product of an entirely secular agenda—the outworking of an institution's legal obligations to its service users or, increasingly, "customers"—with rules of use and access either delegated by the management to the chaplaincy team or left entirely to the chaplains' in/experience, the fact remains that individuals approach the shared space with their own expectations, wrought from membership of a particular faith community. Muslims will not unreasonably expect to find shoe racks and wudu facilities, Christians a cross or crucifix and somewhere to sit, Jews a mezuzah and a pointer to Jerusalem and so on for each faith, as familiar signs or landmarks of being "at home" in "their" place of worship.

The stark truth, though, is that in MFS no one is "at home." Everyone is a "guest" and decidedly not in "their own place of worship." Everyone is an outsider or alien, though free to (choose to) experience a much bigger and more disorienting manifestation of a more inclusive "house of God." For good or ill, the "disturbing presence" of signs of unfamiliarity, or else the "absence of familiarity," together with the lack of what Cummins calls any reassuring sense of the "common time of clocks" (where one worshipper's anticipated Ramadan fast may be contra-posed or even superimposed jarringly upon another's Christmas feast) subverts expectations of a familiar "insider experience" of "at-homeness" with the reality of an "outsider moment," where worshippers of all faiths confront the reality that they are all "strangers" or "sojourners" and that *this* worship space, *this* "house of God" embodies a diversity of faiths and practices that witness ultimately to the radical inclusivity of the presence or reality of the divine in the world.[19]

[18] For example, many Orthodox Jews feel unable to enter the religious spaces of other faiths; many conservative Christian groups shirk spaces that display evidence of use by other faiths; and Baha'i Houses of Worship intentionally offered as "a gift for all people to use for personal prayer and meditation" do not allow communal worship by other faith groups. (https://www.bahai.us/bahai-temple/. Accessed 23/12/16.)
[19] H. Cummins, "Levinas and the Festival of the Cabins," in Kearney and Taylor eds., *Hosting the Stranger: Between Religions* (London: Continuum, 2010), 73–86 at 84.

This in turn firmly locates MFS within the public realm; where multi-faith spaces are revealed as being essentially sites of interaction between strangers and not neighbours, or, perhaps better, sites that offer—for those willing to take the risk—the opportunity to step outside familiarity and the relative "privacy" of safe individual or communal worship space and to engage with strangers. And thereby to experience and perhaps overcome ignorance and stereotyping, in order to help shape and promote the common good and future flourishing of society at large.

For MFS hold the possibility, the capacity, for those who use them, to be an agent for changing personal perspectives on, and religious attitudes towards, those who practice different faiths and hold different world views. For the opportunity for an individual or group to be present during or alongside the worship of another faith—albeit often hidden from view behind a screen—to hear the chants, prayers, murmurings, incantations or cries of someone of a different faith; to witness unfamiliar actions and gestures; *to open oneself to otherness*, to expand one's mental horizons, to confront personal ignorance and communal prejudice and to entertain the possibility of crossing familiar boundaries and limits, making creative interactions and shared new public horizons; to take the risk of imagining a more inclusive and flourishing global human community.[20]

Religious Accommodation in Secular Postcolonial Public Space: Inclusivity or Expediency?

However, while such outcomes remain persuasive for some, it is clear too that the plethora of MFS in the West has very largely emerged not in response to religious ideas or aspirations about shared humanity or religious values, but as the result of five interlinked and quite mundane elements or "drivers":

- the end of colonialism and subsequent new patterns of migration (including political or economic refugees)
- the increased frequency of global travel for both business and pleasure
- the rise of multicultural and multifaith societies (predominantly, though not exclusively, in urban areas) and the consequent debates

---

[20] T. Biddington, "Towards a Theological Reading of Multifaith Spaces," *International Journal of Public Theology*, 7 (2013), 315–328.

around multiculturalism, cosmopolitanism, and the nature of civil society and public theology

- the implementation of Equal Opportunities and Health and Safety legislation
- the attempt to respond to the threat of religiously inspired terrorism by monitoring acts of worship in public spaces

Unsurprisingly, these drivers raise two important questions about motivation. Firstly, whether the presence of MFS embodies a desire on the part of secular governments and administrations to show equal respect to the faiths of all citizens by privileging no one faith or creed over the others, at least within avowedly secular institutions. And secondly, whether the motivation is actually one of expediency: pragmatic, financial/commercial, and social; or something else altogether.

This issue of ambiguous motivation may be illustrated by a situation described by the AHRC project of 2010–2013, where an MFS in a regional British airport was temporarily closed for refurbishment. When travellers requested space to pray, they were directed to an open public space immediately adjacent to the airport security desk. In reality, only the Muslim passengers—obliged to access floor space to pray—were affected by this directive. But here, the various drivers and the questions they raise interconnect and a complex collection of perceptions, motivations, and responses comes into view.

Was this directive based on an assumption by airport security that those (almost exclusively Muslims) praying might be a threat to public safety and so needed close observation? Or that fellow travellers needed to witness the reassuring sight that the security team was doing its job in monitoring those at prayer: Because those (Muslims) at prayer and those (Muslims) committing acts of terror are routinely visibly juxtaposed in the media? And does this then further suggest that the act of praying is harmful to the public good and so needs to take place—like the act of smoking—in designated or restricted areas outside the public purview? (Often in spaces that, because of the relationship between space and financial cost, are located away from prime public seating and commercial vending areas in inconvenient back corridors, adjacent to toilet facilities, service or office areas. Areas that can therefore be further justified as requiring surveillance?)

One could further ask whether the evolution of MFS is as much about pervasive financial/commercial strictures about the construction, allocation, and use of public spaces: why build expensive discrete prayer rooms for multiple faiths when a more cost-effective option is to oblige all faiths to share one space? And to do so in the name of equal opportunities legislation, or community cohesion, or perhaps because of a convenient "theological" view that "everyone worships the same God, anyway"? A view that might be as straightforward an assumption in one way, to a secular mind set, as it may be in another way to (some) people of faith.

MFS: Radical Hospitality or Dangerous Syncretism?

The relationship, in the West, between the evolution of MFS in the public sphere and the requirements of an expedient response to the competing needs of different faiths is manifest. At least in so far as this evolution is driven by secular legislative agendas where MFS are symptomatic of our age: the material consequences of our multi-ethnic society, market economy, individualised religious practice and equality, legislation. In such a world view, MFS merely "house" difference.

However, examples of the phenomenon of religiously motivated MFS offer an alternative story, one where MFS may be an agent of positive social and even theological change, rather than a symptom of the outworking of secular public policy.

One such MFS is the Gaia House Interfaith Center in Carbondale USA (the former Episcopalian Campus House at the University of Southern Illinois) where gather:

> people of many faiths including Muslims, Jews, Hindus, Native Americans, Wiccans, and several Christian denominations … one of the few or only places where an interest group or faith has a physical location to call home … one of the only places in Southern Illinois where so many diverse groups gather openly and freely in one place to engage in dialog and share in community.[21]

Another religiously motivated MFS is the "Tent" interfaith meeting space at St Ethelburga's church in London: "a welcoming, 'liminal' space, standing outside our usual experiences in which new conversations and ways of seeing are possible."[22] Another is the House of Religion in Bern, Switzerland, which houses a reformed Hindu Temple, mosque, Buddhist temple, a

[21] See http://ourgaiahouse.org/our-history. Accessed 14/7/2016.
[22] See https://stethelburgas.org/tent. Accessed 14/7/2016.

church shared between minority Christian groups, and a worship area for Alevis and where Jews, Bahai's, and Sikhs frequently join in activities.[23]

And others are planned. The "House of One" in Berlin is the outworking of discussions between a Protestant Christian minister, a rabbi, and an imam.[24] The "Gods Hus" ("God's House") project in the suburbs of Stockholm where Catholic and Protestant communities have come together to share—not uncontroversially—a single worship space, and where local Muslims plan to build a mosque alongside which will eventually be joined via a shared social space.

And finally, the ambitious *multifaith district* in the suburbs of Paris—housing "two Buddhist temples, a mosque, a synagogue, a Chinese evangelical church and an Armenian cultural centre"—that is being intentionally created to "bring together the citizens of the new town [of Bussy-Saint-Georges]." It is the brainchild of the local mayor who "does not see this concentration [of religious facilities] as a 'religious supermarket,' but rather as an opportunity for people of different faiths to share resources, promote dialogue and enrich the town's cultural life."[25]

While proponents of such multifaith projects are clear about their desire to bring different religions together in the public realm as a sign of mutual endeavour for the common good, detractors emphasise the way in which sharing space relativizes the unique doctrinal claims of discrete religious systems—or, at least, of some systems more than others—and weakens the faith of adherents, confusing them with difference; diluting the values and practices of the established religious community; and promoting "dangerous" syncretistic views and attitudes: perhaps the ultimate spiritual misdemeanour and disregard for self-perpetuating religious orthodoxies and authorities. What, for instance, are Christian and Muslim believers alike to make of a MFS, such as that in Stockholm, designed to accommodate worshippers of one group that believes that Jesus did not die on the cross and of another group that do so believe? What impact does this implicit contradiction have on the nature of religion in the public realm—and (additionally) in a country like the UK where the established faith is Christian? Is it to be an occasion for on-going religious strife or competition? Or is it to be an opportunity for creative dialogue and the attainment of a new place of understanding and co-operation?

[23] http://www.haus-der-religionen.ch/. Accessed 17/7/2016.

[24] See http://house-of-one.org/en. Accessed 15/7/2016.

[25] See https://www.theguardian.com/world/2012/aug/07/religion-faith-district-paris-suburb. Accessed 12/01/17.

MFS as "Cleaving Space"

Clearly viewed from the standpoint of religious orthodoxy that is the hall mark of all established (and therefore "closed" religious systems), MFS are more than potentially risk-filled places. They are essentially destabilising, implicitly contradictory, and to some extent inevitably viewed as "heretical."

In this way they serve both to mirror and effect the change that has occurred in the public face of religion in the postcolonial West: by intentionally creating space—and thus mimicking contemporary "sacroscapes" (to use Tweed's phrase)—in which people of different religions overlap, overhear, and oversee the "practices of otherness."[26] Moreover, post-empire, MFS refuse or subvert any endeavour at circumscription we might have by our attempts to create or privilege particular preformed or tribal "places" or "texts"—religious and spiritual identities—of our own and offer instead (again to reference Tweed) places of 'flux, transition and crossing.'[27]

For MFS are "cleaving spaces": suggesting that they embody both the centrifugal "splitting or forcing apart" of what is "abject," or "viscerally incompatible" and to be cast out—in the form of contradictory belief—and, at the same time, the centripetal "cleaving together" of what is alike and desires union, in the form of shared "religious belief" in a secular (and alleged non-believing) world. In other words, they may be deemed "houses to syncretism" by some, while others may view them both as the "creative refuge" into which religion retreats in the secular institutional sphere, and also as the potential future birthplace (the womb) of a new vision for the future. For they are places that are designed to *appear empty*, by virtue of the absence of the anticipated religious symbology of any one faith, but which contain the seed for some still undefined and inchoate future potential for humanity.[28] Like the *anchorages* of medieval England, where visionaries and mystics withdrew, so as to better seek the will of God, today's MFS are places that are pregnant with possibility.[29]

---

[26] T.A. Tweed, *Crossing and Dwelling. A Theory of Religion* (Cambridge, MA: Harvard University Press, 2006).

[27] Ibid.

[28] Andrew Crompton, "The Architecture of Multifaith Spaces: God Leaves the Building," *The Journal of Architecture* (2013). https://doi.org/10.1080/13602365.2013.821149.

[29] From the Greek *ana* "back" and *khorein* "withdraw, give place," and *khoros* "place, space, free space."

THEOLOGICAL SIGNIFICANCE

In their examination of the discovery—no doubt both disturbing and enlightening in equal measure—that, God's sacredness could be found outside of Israel, in exile (and not as originally believed), the early rabbis taught that this "outside the Temple" sacredness needed "to be activated."[30] That people could indeed discover God's sacred presence to be wherever they were; but that this discovery was *dependent upon intentional activity.* It needed, and it needs, to be sought and recognised. And then the site of this discovery then becomes "an arena which partakes of the qualities of that which dwells there."[31] The space itself is transformed and becomes, as it were, God-filled, or filled with divine possibility. No matter where it is located.

In the terminology of Bachelard, such resonant, divinely charged space becomes "felicitous."[32] For it allows those so minded to see such space/s disclosing new realities and revealing new possibilities for God's presence and action in the world, in the form of multiple communities, cultures and faiths, as well as new opportunities for creative human interaction.

But for this to happen, Lilburne emphasises, "theology must surrender one-dimensional notions of truth ... [to create] a new appreciation of the ... logics of implication and intuition which have been widely ignored in traditional theological methodology."[33] For the MFS issue, the challenge, to believers and non-believers alike, is to see God's kingdom as "ultimately inclusive."[34] Or, to reference the famous phrase in John's Gospel (14:2), "in my father's house are many mansions [or rooms]." Thus, one clear urgent and practical challenge to theologians is to see MFS as a mechanism for the shaping of theologies that include alterity as a matter of principle, a place to begin. Indeed, to recognise that, human redemption may be found along the road that leads to the creation of such inclusive theologies.

MFS also challenge theologians and believers of all faiths to understand that, in the secular realm at least, MFS witness—as the sociologist of reli-

---

[30] Baruch M. Bokser, "Approaching Sacred Space," *Harvard Theological Review* 78 (1985), 279–299. Cited in Geoffrey R. Lilburne, *A Sense of Place: A Christian Theology of the Land* (Nashville: Abingdon Press, 1989), 69.

[31] Lilburne, *A Sense of Place*, 72.

[32] Gaston Bachelard, *The Poetics of Space* (trans. Maria Jolas) (Boston: Beacon Press, 1969).

[33] Lilburne, *A Sense of Place*, 82.

[34] Lilburne, *A Sense of Place*, 102.

gion Peter L Berger points out—to the way in which religions have been "replaced by ways of dealing with the world *etsi Deus non daretur*": as if God did not exist.[35] That this "pragmatic atheism," rooted in the ideas of the seventeenth century Dutch jurist Hugo Grotius, is a necessary and creative response to the presence of the competing claims of multiple religions in an ever shrinking world. And that, as such, MFS offer a "formula of peace" (Berger's phrase) or, in architectural parlance, "spaces for peace," that address the need not only for the political but for the *theological* understanding and management of pluralism. And not only between the secular and sacred worlds, and between the different world faiths, but also between the current and future manifestations of divine and human action in the world.

CONCLUSION

Yet, whether devised by secular non-religious motivation, driven by religious desire for interfaith co-operation and collaboration, or as a means to manage the equilibrium between contemporary experiences of pluralism, MFS hint at a postcolonial and postmodern utopia that is being birthed in our world. A world where strangers become sojourners, companions sharing bread, and where the human and the divine together can create seemingly empty, but ineluctably (re-)generative spaces fit for inspiring the prophetic action that enables future human understanding and co-operating, and—who knows?—for shaping future stages of human social and evolutionary consciousness.

BIBLIOGRAPHY

Bachelard, Gaston. 1969. *The Poetics of Space.* Trans. Maria Jolas. Boston: Beacon Press.

Biddington, T. 2013. Towards a Theological Reading of Multifaith Spaces. *International Journal of Public Theology 7.*

Bokser, Baruch M. 1985. Approaching Sacred Space. *Harvard Theological Review* 78: 279–299.

Bowman, G. 2010. Orthodox-Muslim Interactions at 'Mixed Shrines' in Macedonia. In *Eastern Christians in Anthropological Perspective,* ed. Chris Hann and Hermann Goltz. California: University of California Press.

---

[35] Peter L. Berger, *The Many Altars of Modernity. Towards a Paradigm for Religion in a Pluralist Age* (Boston/Berlin: De Gruyter, 2014).

Brand, R., A. Crompton, C. Hewson, and T. Biddington. 2010–2013. Multi-Faith Spaces: Symptoms and Agents of Religious and Social Change. *AHRC Religion and Society Programme*, AH/H017321/1.
Cadge, Wendy. 2013. *Paging God: Religion in the Halls of Medicine*. Chicago: University of Chicago Press.
Crompton, Andrew. 2013. The Architecture of Multifaith Spaces: God Leaves the Building. *The Journal of Architecture* 18: 474–496.
Cummins, H. 2010. Levinas and the Festival of the Cabins. In *Hosting the Stranger: Between Religions*, ed. Richard Kearney and James Taylor. London: Continuum.
Emmett, C. 2009. The Siting of Churches and Mosques as an Indicator of Christian-Muslim Relations. *Islam and Christian-Muslim Relations* 20 (4): 451–476.
Klanten, Robert, and Lukas Feireiss, eds. 2010. *Closer to God: Religious Architecture and Sacred Spaces*. Berlin: Gestalten.
Lilburne, Geoffrey R. 1989. *A Sense of Place: A Christian Theology of the Land*. Nashville: Abingdon Press.
Mohammad, Afsar. 2013. *The Festival of Pirs: Popular Islam and Shared Devotion in South India*. Oxford: Oxford University Press.
Sikand, Yoginder. 2003. *Sacred Spaces: Exploring Traditions of Shared Faith in India*. New Delhi: Penguin Books India.
Tweed, T.A. 2006. *Crossing and Dwelling: A Theory of Religion*. Cambridge, MA: Harvard University Press.

REFERENCES TO ONLINE SOURCES

Azad, Shivani. 2016. Tarun Vijay, Dalits Pelted with Stone for Defying Temple Ban. *The Times of India*, July 14. http://timesofindia.indiatimes.com/india/Tarun-Vijay-Dalits-pelted-with-stone-for-defying-temple-ban/articleshow/52367193.cms.
Birla Mandir Jaipur, History, Facts and Story of Birla Temple. *Indialine: Complete India Travel Guide*. Accessed 19 July 2016. http://www.indialine.com/travel/rajasthan/jaipur/birla-temple.html.
DNA Web Team. 2016. Five Places of Worship in India That Deny Entry to Women. *Daily News and Analysis India*, April 1. Accessed 14 July 2016. http://www.dnaindia.com/india/report-shani-temple-sabarimala-sree-padmanabhaswamy-haji-ali-entry-to-women-2196954.
Dom St. Petri Bautzen. *Marketing-Gesellschaft Oberlausitz-Niederschlesien mbH*. Accessed 23 November 2016. http://www.oberlausitz.com/ferien/kulturell/via-sacra/de/dom-st.petri-domschatzkammer-bautzen.aspx.
Epiphany Cathedral. *Find Messages*. Accessed 19 July 2016. http://www.findmessages.com/tag/epiphany-cathedral.

Haus der religionen-Dialog der kulturen. *Haus der religionen.* Accessed 17 July 2016. http://www.haus-der-religionen.ch/.

House of One. *House of One.* Accessed 15 July 2016. http://house-of-one.org/en.

Le Bars, Stéphanie. 2012. Bussy-Saint-Georges, the Town with Built-in Religious Harmony. *The Guardian,* August 7. Accessed 12 January 2017. https://www.theguardian.com/world/2012/aug/07/religion-faith-district-paris-suburb.

Make the Chapel Your Own. 2016. *Rothko Chapel,* July 14. http://rothkochapel.org/experience/private-services/.

Our History. *Gaia House Interfaith Center.* Accessed 14 July 2016. http://our-gaiahouse.org/our-history.

Prayer Room. 2016. *Vienna Airport,* November 23. http://www.viennaairport.com/en/passengers/airport/prayer_room.

The Bahá'í House of Worship for North America. *National Spiritual Assembly of the Bahá'ís of the United States.* Accessed 23 December 2016. https://www.bahai.us/bahai-temple/.

Venue Hire. *St Ethelburga's.* Accessed 14 July 2016. https://stethelburgas.org/tent.

CHAPTER 4

Remembering Together: Co-Memoration in Northern Ireland

Jonathan Dunn

INTRODUCTION

Co-Memoration: Remembering Together as Living Together

When the conference which birthed this volume gathered in Manchester in May of 2016, it confronted again the challenges of '*Living together* after Empire'. In this vein, the chapters of this volume, in different contexts and in different ways, continue that effort. This chapter does so by addressing one particular aspect of living together, the challenge of remembering together. Specifically, it will consider how a society divided by conflict might remember that conflict *together*. That is to say, this chapter is concerned with the task of commemoration, and a particular understanding of commemoration at that. For, as this chapter will show, commemoration, and its associated environments and practices, has the potential to exclude as well as include. In pursuit of a way of truly *living together* after

J. Dunn (✉)
Department of Theology & Religious Studies, University of Chester, Chester, UK
e-mail: j.dunn@chester.ac.uk

© The Author(s) 2019
J. Dunn et al. (eds.), *Multiple Faiths in Postcolonial Cities*, Postcolonialism and Religions,
https://doi.org/10.1007/978-3-030-17144-5_4

Empire, this chapter, following the approach of the paper it is based upon, identifies some of the issues which make a genuinely co-memorative remembrance of conflict difficult in the context of contemporary Northern Ireland.

The Context: Remembering Together in Northern Ireland

The ceasefires announced by the main paramilitary organisations in the mid-1990s have led to a marked decrease in, although not quite a total cessation of, the sectarian violence which erupted in 1969. Furthermore, the ratification of the Belfast Agreement of 1998, the implementation of subsequent agreements, and the establishment and re-establishment of political institutions where power has been shared between unionist and nationalists represent further attempts to facilitate a transition to a post-conflict society.[1] While the collapse of the power-sharing institutions in January 2017, and the failure to reach an agreement which would see them re-established, has demonstrated the fragility of the political process, it is the wider social context which has been the focus of long-standing concerns. These concerns have persisted even through times of relative optimism about the sustainability of the political arrangements. Published before the collapse of the institutions in 2016, the latest *Northern Ireland Peace Monitoring Report*, while stating that 'Northern Ireland's political institutions had become more stable', expressed concerns about the persistence of entrenched divisions within society.[2] Included among the 'ten key points' in the report is the conclusion that 'How Northern Ireland deals with its troubled past remains to be resolved'.[3] Viewed in this context, the challenge of remembering together can be seen as central to a wider challenge, that of moving on from armistice towards reconciliation. As such, while remembering the conflict together as a society remains largely a future, and perhaps distant, goal of peace-making in Northern Ireland, it is a pressing concern.

The remembrance of conflict was subject to a renewal of interest across the island of Ireland at the time of writing, in the middle of what has come to be known as a 'Decade of Centenaries'. This term refers to

---

[1] 'The Belfast Agreement' is also known as 'The Good Friday Agreement'.

[2] Robin Wilson, *Northern Ireland Peace Monitoring Report*, Number Four, September 2016, Northern Ireland Community Relations Council.

[3] Ibid., p. 13.

the anniversaries of key events within that turbulent and formative period in Irish history from 1912 to 1922. In fact, our conference fell between two of the most emotive of those centenaries. It came shortly after the commemoration of 'the Rising' against British forces in the Easter of 1916, an event which continues to hold particular significance for republicans and nationalists across Ireland. In addition, our conference occurred prior to the 1st of July commemorations of the World War I Battle of the Somme, a battle which is primarily remembered by unionists for the resulting decimation of the 36th (Ulster) Division of the British army.

In the midst of this decade of centenaries, and between these two most emotive anniversaries in particular, it seemed that, more than ever before, commemoration was a topic of discussion across Ireland. Furthermore, commemoration had not only become subject to greater interest, but to sustained critical reflection. Indeed, the Easter Rising and Battle of the Somme commemorations were the subject of a series of conferences and events across the island. Many of these were organised by religious denominations. One such initiative, 'The Future of Our Past: Remembering and Reassessing 1916' was organised by The Presbyterian Church in Ireland's Union Theological College at Queen's University Belfast. The conference and subsequent seminars have been part of a wider initiative to open up a meaningful conversation about how Irish society on both sides of the border might work together for the common good in the context of different understandings of the past. Notably, of some 350 people who attended the conference, faith leaders from the different traditions were present and all varieties and shades of political opinion were represented.[4] Endeavours such as 'The Future of Our Past' signal recognition, at least on the part of those involved, that a willingness to remember together is indeed essential to a peace which includes, and fosters, reconciliation. What is more, the initiative shown by churches and theological colleges in stimulating and facilitating dialogue in this area signals recognition, on their part at least, that Christian theology has a role to play in the pursuit of this public good.

---

[4] Information about the conference 'The Future of our Past' and video recordings of its sessions can be accessed at http://www.presbyterianireland.org/News/2016-News-Archive/February-2016/The-Church-in-the-Public-Square-The-Future-of-Our.aspx.

The Scale of the Challenge

Such initiatives however, represent but a start. Indeed, the observation that meaningful dialogue is just beginning to address how the events of 100 years ago should be commemorated says much about the lack of progress in this area. It is also sounds a note of caution regarding the ambitions of a chapter such as this one. Serious difficulties in commemorating beyond the 1914–1918 and 1939–1945 wars, in particular commemorating post-1969 conflict, persist, as do attempts to address them.[5] The existence and nature of such difficulties will be illustrated in due course through engagement with individual examples. The scale of the challenge however, can be made clear here at the outset, when we grasp the order of the questions being wrestled with. For the obstacles to be overcome are exemplified not so much in questions such as 'can we remember combatants motivated by ideas and allegiances we have long identified as opposed to our own'? but in prior questions concerning the very nature of the conflict itself. The question of who might be termed 'combatants' and the related one of whether some might be termed 'criminals' remains unsettled and divisive. Ultimately, these questions are concerned with the legitimacy of, at least some of, the violence. They are questions which therefore have the potential to determine who and what are included and excluded from public remembrance. Yet, they remain, also, questions which Christian theology cannot swerve, however inconvenient they may prove in the pursuit of inclusive remembrance. For many, not least those who have suffered as a result of the conflict, questions of legitimacy are inextricably linked to a desire for justice. A Christian theology which is worthy of the name cannot jettison concerns with justice voiced from any quarter. Rather, in sharing a desire for justice, it must seek truth and reconciliation by, at least, suggesting appropriate approaches to these issues.

[5] Representatives from faith communities have been at the forefront of recent efforts to engage with and address these difficulties publicly through the mainstream media and other channels. The proposal of a 'Day of Acknowledgement' by the former President of the Methodist Church in Ireland, Harold Good, stands as a recent example of this. As reported by BBC News, the suggestion that 'Together across our community we might come together each of us and all of us, from all sectors including the churches and acknowledge our part in the hurt the grief and the pain of the past 48 plus years' received 'guarded support' from many other church representatives. http://www.bbc.co.uk/news/uk-northern-ireland-40991758 accessed 22 August 2017.

Approaching the Issues

The approach taken by this chapter draws on post-colonial methodologies and resources from within the field of Christian public theology. At this point, it should be acknowledged that applying post-colonial methods to contemporary Northern Ireland is not uncontroversial. Any reading of this context which classifies the situation as 'post-colonial', or implies such a classification, risks alienating key constituencies at the outset. Whilst some may object that the situation in the north of Ireland is not *post-*colonial at all, but colonial, given that much of north of the island remains British in terms of its constitutional status, others may react against the implications of the '-colonial' element of this label, not least because of the implications for their own identity.

Given that this volume aims to reflect on how people might live together, and this chapter aims to reflect on how people might remember together, the potentially divisive impact of post-colonial terminology is a considerable risk. While these risks are acknowledged, and the difficulties which give rise to it are recognised, I would contend that they do not necessarily precipitate an impasse here. Rather I would suggest that, while the term itself may have a divisive impact if applied as a label to the context, approaching this issue of remembering together in light of the insights of post-colonial approaches to other contexts may provide a way forward. As F.C. McGrath points out, whilst 'the designation of Ireland, north or south, as postcolonial has been resisted by many in Ireland as well as by many postcolonial critics… Nonetheless, more than eight centuries of colonization have left Ireland, north and south, with features of a post-colonial legacy that resemble those in other formerly colonized countries'.[6] Many of these resemblances can be recognised even by those who would not follow McGrath's characterisation of the past eight centuries of Irish history. As such, the approach I am advocating does not assume parallels and relevance across contexts, but takes an open and discerning attitude to what can be learnt from other situations. In paying particular attention to how the commemoration of conflict in this context may effectively exclude and marginalise, this chapter employs a self-consciously post-colonial method.

---

[6] F.C. McGrath, 'Settler Nationalism: Ulster Unionism and Postcolonial Theory', *Irish Studies Review*, 2012, p. 465.

As I have noted above, the decade of centenaries has seen many Christian denominations and theologians in this context participate in efforts, engage and encourage public dialogue on these issues. This chapter approaches the issue from the perspective of a public theology which commends these, and further, initiatives.[7] However, public theology offers to do much more than that: It is essential to ensuring that these efforts remain informed and accountable.

In *God for a Secular Society: The Public Relevance of Theology*, Jürgen Moltmann describes how he understands the public role of Christian theology:

> Its subject alone makes Christian theology a *theologica publica*... It gets involved in the public affairs of society. It thinks about what is of general concern in the light of hope in Christ for the kingdom of God. It becomes political in the name of the poor and the marginalized in a given society. Remembrance of the crucified Christ makes it critical towards political religions and idolatries. It thinks critically about the religious and moral values of the societies in which it exists, and presents its reflections as a reasoned position.[8]

Public theology, as advocated by Moltmann here, demands that Christian theology speaks into situations such as the challenge of remembering together in Northern Ireland. In Moltmann's view, Christian theology is already inextricably involved. Surely, some reconciling word is to be offered in Christ's name, some exhortation to remember together sounded, some guidance given to those who would answer that call. Concern with doing just this has no doubt motivated, and continues to motivate, those who took the recent centenaries as an opportunity for theological dialogue. In doing so they reiterate that their Christian theologies claim for themselves an undeniably *public* role. Indeed, on Moltmann's reading, it would seem that a theology which neglects such a task in this context would arguably not be much of a theology at all, detached as it

---

[7] An example of such a further initiative is the Presbyterian Church in Ireland's 'Reconciliation through Dealing with the Past: Learning from Presbyterian Responses to the Troubles'. At the time of writing, this academic research project was being developed in partnership with Queen's University Belfast, with the support of the Irish Department of Foreign Affairs Reconciliation Fund.

[8] Jürgen Moltmann, *God for a Secular Society: The Public Relevance of Theology*. London: SCM Press, 1999, p. 1.

would be from a reconciling *Theos*. Furthermore, it can hardly be Christian theology, distant as it would be from the example of the reconciling Christ.

Not only does Moltmann's vision of Christian theology as public theology motivate engagement with the issues, but it points to the resources by which that engagement is to be kept informed, critical and accountable. For while such a theology must approach what is of general concern, the public remembrance of conflict in this case, it must also take care to do so 'in the light of hope in Christ for the kingdom of God'. 'It becomes political' not with freedom to choose its own interests or adopt the interests of one socio-economic or ethnic group but 'in the name of the poor and the marginalized in a given society'. It is on this basis that my approach will exhibit a concern with the marginalising effects of current practices and beliefs surrounding the commemoration of conflict. Equally, on Moltmann's reading, public theology is 'critical towards political religions and idolatries', which may be complicit in that marginalisation. That critical attitude must also extend to the very 'religious and moral values of the societies in which it exists'.[9] It is on this basis that attention will be paid to the factors which underpin current forms of commemoration in this chapter.

Keeping Faith with the Dead

'Since when is forgiveness a better quality than loyalty?' So asks the character Roger Sterling in an episode of the television series 'Madmen', when, as a US navy veteran, he struggles to contemplate doing business with a Japanese company some two decades after the 1945 cessation of hostilities between the two countries.[10] The loyalty he refers to is, specifically, his loyalty to the friends he lost in combat with Japanese forces. The forgiveness he refers to is, specifically, both a requirement for doing business with people to whom he attributes some indirect responsibility for that loss, and the implication of doing so. This fictional character's question no doubt reflects the real dilemmas faced by some of those whose factual circumstances are mirrored in the plot of this episode. There is relevance too beyond the context of that particular conflict, for it undoubtedly comes close to the heart of the dilemma faced by many in Northern Ireland today. In this context, the tension is between a sense of loyalty to

[9] Ibid.
[10] Madmen Season 4 Episode 5, 'The Chrysanthemum and the Sword', AMC, 2010.

friends and loved ones lost, and the forgiveness required for, and implied by, more inclusive commemoration.

It is just this sense of loyalty, albeit in its most extreme form, that the Canadian historian Michael Ignatieff describes as 'a desire to keep faith with the dead'. In his book, *The Warrior's Honor: Ethnic War and the Modern Conscience*, Ignatieff explored what motivated revenge in the context of Serbia, Croatia, Bosnia, Rwanda and Afghanistan in the mid-1990s. His conclusion was that because 'revenge is commonly regarded as a low and unworthy emotion... its deep moral hold on people is rarely understood. But revenge morally considered—is a desire to keep faith with the dead, to honour their memory by taking up their cause where they left off'.[11]

There is of course, a significant difference between a desire for revenge and a sense that it would be inappropriate for one to take part in a particular act of commemoration. Yet, while it was witnessing the former which gave caused Ignatieff to recognise the keeping of faith with the dead, it may also to be observed in cases of the latter. In such cases however, Ignatieff's formulation requires an adjustment; it is, perhaps, better expressed in negative form. For, the problem is not so much a desire to keep faith with the dead, but a fear of betraying the dead. It is this concern that is often in tension with the desire for reconciliation. Such a concern which might prevent one from joining with others in remembering a conflict or event, because who or what is included or excluded from the memory being publicly expressed constitutes a betrayal of the dead and wounded one calls one's own.

From this question of loyalty and forgiveness, the question of justice is never far away. In so many cases, and hence for so many people, the question of justice remains unresolved. With so many answers, convictions, apologies outstanding, fear of betraying the dead through inappropriate commemoration is not an abstract or unfounded proposition. 'The deep moral hold', Ignatieff describes, is all the deeper for this sense of injustice.[12] All the more reason then that these concerns cannot be viewed as an inconvenience in the path towards more inclusive commemoration, and reconciliation more generally, to be eliminated or eroded over time.

[11] Michael Ignatieff, *The Warrior's Honor: Ethnic War and the Modern Conscience.* New York: Henry Holt, 1997, p. 188.
[12] Ibid.

Indeed, viewed theologically, the outstanding answers, convictions, apologies might be understood as amounting to respective deficits of truth, justice and repentance in the current context. Such deficits no doubt add greatly to the cost of forgiveness for those affected by them.

JAMES MCLEAN: A CASE STUDY

Among those who have experienced difficulties with commemorating the more recent past, few have had more attention given to their objections than James Mclean. Mclean, at the time of writing, a professional footballer for West Bromwich Albion, a club in the English Premier League (EPL), has repeatedly opted out of wearing an embroidered poppy on his kit, as is traditional for players in the EPL on the game nearest to Remembrance Day.[13]

Mclean's explanation of his refusal to wear a poppy is an insight into the nature of the considerations at play in this context:

> If the poppy was simply about World War One and Two victims alone, I'd wear it without a problem…. I would wear it every day of the year if that was the thing but it doesn't, it stands for all the conflicts that Britain has been involved in. Because of the history where I come from in Derry, I cannot wear something that represents that.[14]

On one level, this statement is simply further evidence that where difficulties arise with current forms of public commemoration, these difficulties tend to centre on the inclusion of the period known as 'the Troubles'. Yet, with further reflection, Mclean's words here actually afford insight into the very nature of these difficulties. The way in which Mclean explains his actions points to a localised loyalty as the motivating factor: It is 'because of the history [of] where I come from in Derry'.[15] For Mclean, it seems that ultimately, it is loyalty to a community, rather than allegiance to a flag or a state, that discourages him from wearing a commemorative

---

[13] Having been present at one such game at Old Trafford in November 2015, when Mclean was the only player to appear without a poppy for West Bromwich Albion against Manchester United, I can testify to the hostility with which his protest has been met, even in Great Britain.

[14] http://www.birminghammail.co.uk/sport/football/football-news/james-mcclean-remembrance-day-poppy-12075538 accessed February 2017. From an original interview given to *Albion News*. The Official West Bromwich Albion Matchday Programme, 2015.

[15] Ibid.

poppy. Taken at face value then, Mclean's explanation roots his objection in his identification with, and sense of loyalty to, the community in which he originated.

Whilst Mclean here cites the history of where he comes from in general terms, rather than specifying one event, the proximity of his childhood home in Creggan, inner city 'Derry', to the scene of 'Bloody Sunday' is indicative of the type of impact the conflict may have had on the experiences of his community.[16] Given the dramatic scale of such events, relative to the compact scale of such communities, it may be appropriate to understand this community loyalty in the even more localised terms of family and personal loyalty. This type of desire to keep faith with one's own wounded and bereaved community is often itself rooted in and inseparable from a desire to keep faith with wounded, bereaved, even deceased, individuals known, perhaps known well; friends, and friends of family, even relatives.

REMEMBRANCE SUNDAY: ANECDOTES OF ABSENCE IN A FAITH COMMUNITY

Whilst Mclean's issues with current forms of national commemoration are publicly recorded and widely known across the United Kingdom and Ireland, the post-colonial approach of this chapter means that it must shift the focus to the less often heard stories of those on the margins. Specifically, we shift our attentions to the experience of those who may find themselves on the margins of their faith community through their experience of commemorative alienation. Just what is meant by commemorative alienation can be illustrated by examples from my personal recollection of church attendance in a Protestant congregation in Northern Ireland. For, every Remembrance Sunday that passed in this particular congregation, two families were, I came to realise over a number of years, regularly absent. They were otherwise regular attenders, who were present virtually every Sunday, except Remembrance Sunday. Their absence was not to be explained, like that of others, by their participation in a civic service at the local cenotaph. Rather, it appears to lie in the fact that within each of these families at least one member had been a raised in the Roman Catholic tradition.

---

[16] An introductory section of *The Report of the Bloody Sunday Inquiry* (London: The Stationery Office, 2010) refers to its subject in the following way: 'The loss of life' which occurred 'in connection with the civil rights march in Londonderry on 30th January 1972. Thirteen civilians were killed by Army gunfire on the day. The day has become generally known as Bloody Sunday'. Volume 1, p. 45.

The significance of these anecdotes of absence is that while their regular presence in a Protestant place of worship suggested changes in their religious identification and beliefs, their annual absence may suggest that changes in their religious belief and identity did not coincide with, or result in, a transformation in the myriad other loyalties and allegiances bound up with their identity and their narrative of the conflict. Religious conversion did not bring political conversion, and why should it? Ostensibly, these were not politically active people, this was not some defiant show of keeping faith with the dead, but evidently there was discomfort, unease, a sense of awkwardness, perhaps a fear of betrayal. Reflecting on this from the distance of several years, their absence spoke to me, not of a disconnection between their allegiances, but a disconnection between the space and liturgy of the worship and the theology that ought to guide it.

My assumptions may, of course, be well off the mark. If any interpretation of their absence ought to be privileged, it is their own. It is, then, necessary that those who choose to stay away from their place of worship on Remembrance Sunday are encouraged to voice their reasons for doing so. It is essential that they continue to have a voice in the dialogue towards a more inclusive way of remembering. What is more, these observations from my experience are undeniably anecdotal. Without systematic surveys of similar absences and attitudes, the issue of whether they reflect a wider trend is open to speculation. Such a survey is beyond the bounds of this chapter; however, this chapter aims to underline the need for them. Only then can the full range of reasons for absences and the true scale of the challenge be appreciated.

Even in the anecdotal form they take here however, these stories from the margins, suggest that the issues related to commemoration require a theological response. That response must not only be 'public' in the sense Moltmann speaks of, in the sense of 'getting involved in the public affairs of society', but by virtue of reflecting critically on an area which is, I would argue, no less 'public' in its own way, that of public worship, of space and liturgy.[17] What this chapter can and does offer then, is a reflection on the ways in which particular narratives of the conflict are embodied in features of the worship space, and voiced in aspects of the liturgy. It should be noted that the situations referred to reflect my own personal experience in so far as they are primarily examples of Protestant places of worship and liturgies, predominantly those of the Presbyterian Church in Ireland and the (Anglican) Church of Ireland.

[17] Moltmann, God for a Secular Society, p. 1.

EMBODIED NARRATIVES: PHYSICAL SYMBOLS IN WORSHIP SPACES

As those who have spent time within Protestant worship spaces in Northern Ireland will have noticed, the vast majority of these spaces contain physical symbols which express national, military and personal connections. While most, if not all, of these physical symbols remain on display within the worship space throughout the year and not just during services involving the commemoration of conflict, their presence is nonetheless commemorative of conflict. Indeed, in many cases, that will have been the intention of their placement in the worship space and continues to be their recognised function within the life of the congregation meeting there. To explain, and explore further, exactly what type of physical symbols are meant and the current effects of their presence, I have grouped them into three categories: 'flags', 'emblems' and 'memorials'.

Flags

While there is an overlap between flags and emblems, in that many flags hanging in these spaces bear the emblems of organisations, the category 'flags' is here restricted to those of nations and regions. Those which denote affiliation with organisations will be considered under the heading 'emblems'. This approach is necessary, given that the threefold categorisation I am employing here is largely concerned with the narratives embodied and their effect, rather than the physical form of the symbol.

In the main, where a national flag is displayed within a Protestant place of worship, it is almost invariably, and exclusively, the flag of the United Kingdom of Great Britain and Ireland, known variously and interchangeably as the Union flag or Union jack. These flags are in some cases overlaid with military insignia; however, as noted above, it is the effect of the national identification which is to be considered here. While the identification of a place of worship with any marker of national identity may present difficulties for some Christians in principle, there are a number of potential difficulties which are specific to this context. On one level, there is the contested constitutional status of Northern Ireland. The principle of consent enshrined in the Belfast Agreement of 1998, and preserved by subsequent agreements, ensures that Northern Ireland remains part of the United Kingdom so long as this remains the will of the people of Northern

Ireland.[18] In addition, individual citizens within Northern Ireland have the right to either British or Irish nationality.[19] Thus, while the presence of a Union Jack in the worship space reflects the constitutional status quo and the national identity of some who are regularly in attendance, for those who do not share that national identity and who may desire a change in the constitutional status quo to reflect their own identity, the flag's presence may have the effect of asserting the marginality of their identity within their worship community. The marginalising effect of a marker of national identity which is other to their own may also be exacerbated by the absence of a marker of their own national identity.

In the context of commemoration, these considerations may at first be deemed incidental. This chapter is not primarily concerned with the marginalising effects of expressions of national identity in themselves. Such a conclusion also appears to be encouraged by the assertion of this chapter that the key difficulties in relation to commemoration are rooted in loyalties operative at the localised levels of community, family and personal connections. However, to conclude that the difficulties posed by the presence of flags are incidental here would be to ignore the connections between localised loyalties and national identities. Given the identification of many of those involved in the conflict with British or Irish nationality, markers of one or other of these national identities can bring about remembrances of those involved in or caught up in the conflict, and their actions or experiences. The effect of such remembrances is often dependant on the nature of one's localised loyalties. Symbols of British identity may be difficult to disentangle from the memory of a friend, neighbour or loved one killed by someone

[18] The Belfast Agreement affirms this principle in these terms: 'it is for the people of the island of Ireland alone, by agreement between the two parts respectively and without external impediment, to exercise their right of self-determination on the basis of consent, freely and concurrently given, North and South, to bring about a united Ireland, if that is their wish, accepting that this right must be achieved and exercised with and subject to the agreement and consent of a majority of the people of Northern Ireland.' 'Constitutional Issues' 1.ii, *The Belfast Agreement*, Northern Ireland Office, Belfast, 1998, p. 3. https://www.gov.uk/government/uploads/system/uploads/attachment_data/file/136652/agreement.pdf accessed 22 August 2017.

[19] The agreement also recognises 'the birthright of all the people of Northern Ireland to identify themselves and be accepted as Irish or British, or both, as they may so choose, and accordingly confirm[s] that their right to hold both British and Irish citizenship is accepted by both Governments and would not be affected by any future change in the status of Northern Ireland. 'Article 1.vi', *The Belfast Agreement*, p. 33.

purporting to act on behalf of the British people, just as symbols of Irish identity may be difficult to disentangle from the memory of a friend, neighbour or loved one killed by someone purporting to act on behalf of the Irish people.

Emblems

Even where no emblem is emblazoned on a national flag, the effect then may be little different. While, of course, a flag as a marker of national identity is intended to have a wider symbolism than the actions of those who lay claim to it in any particular way, in this context, its primary symbolism for those who have been affected by the conflict may be an association with a particular organisation, and the actions of that organisation in relation to one(s) known by them. However, where emblems representing various branches of the security forces are displayed, the intended effect is to encourage the recollection of the actions and experiences of their membership. On at least one level, the desire to have such emblems in a place of worship is entirely understandable. Their presence encourages and facilitates the commemoration of the actions and experiences of members of that worshipping community, past and present, and their colleagues. These are actions and experiences which many within that community, not least those with personal or family connections to the organisation, will interpret as being honourable, sacrificial and undoubtedly worthy of public remembrance. However, in the wider context of a society where experiences of contact with participants in the conflict varied, as did understandings of the role of these participants, this interpretation is not uncontested.

Memorials

These difficulties come into even sharper focus when attention is paid to the presence of personal memorials to those killed by paramilitary organisations within many Protestant worship spaces in Northern Ireland. As with the erection and maintenance of emblems, this is an understandable expression of the desire to commemorate those profoundly affected by the conflict within a particular community. It is also understandable that these memorials should bear a wording which reflects a particular interpretation of the conflict within the narrative chosen by those who erected it. Examples such as 'murdered by terrorists' or 'murdered by cowards' illustrate how these memorials communicate a narrative about the legitimacy of aspects of the conflict which would be contested in the region.[20]

The Possibility of Neutral Space

It should be noted that a small number of attempts have been made to instigate the removal of physical symbols such as those described above, with such moves usually focussing on flags, perhaps given the more explicitly personal nature of emblems and memorials. Where such moves have been made, they do not suggest that moves towards neutral worship spaces are an immediate prospect. The two cases known to me—one the anonymised recollection of a minister, the other reported in the regional press—illustrate how when those particular church leaders sought to neutralise the space, they found the enterprise to be a painful and fruitless one. In one case, a minister who saw an opportunity to create a worship space free from flags and emblems in the move to a new church building saw his motion to do so voted down by the congregation's ruling body. His response, personally carrying the flags into the new church building himself contrasts with another case, as widely reported at the time, where flags and emblems were removed from a church building apparently without the required permission.[21]

The Advisability of Neutral Space

The question of the possibility of 'neutralising' the spaces, suggests a prior question of whether it is in fact advisable; a question which itself is inextricable from a collection of sensitive and emotive dilemmas. Can spaces which do not reflect the historical and cultural setting of the congregation be considered an improvement on the current state of affairs? Can existing memorials to deceased individuals be removed or altered without implying betrayal and provoking offence? Would doing so actually result in a more neutral space, or would it rather embody an alternative, equally alienating, narrative in the space now empty or reoccupied?

[20] Given the sensitivity of such memorials, it would be inappropriate to make reference to any one example. Their existence is not disputed and evidence of this type of wording is commonplace.

[21] BBC News Northern Ireland, 'Minister resigns after removing British Legion flags', http://www.bbc.co.uk/news/uk-northern-ireland-34604227 Published 22 October 2015, Accessed 23 August 2017.

The difficulties inherent in moving to a space devoid of these physical symbols are most evident in relation to memorials. Whilst the significance of these memorials is congregational, communal, collegial, as well as familial, and personal, those for whom these memorials have a personal and family significance must be considered key stakeholders in any discussion of their continuing place within the life of the congregation. From their perspective, any suggestion that an existing memorial is removed or modified may well have offensive implications. Among such implications may be the suggestion that events might not have happened in the way they understand them, or that the significance of events may be otherwise understood. In such circumstances, even attempts to neutralise the worship space appears bound to result in privileging the narratives of one constituency over another. To have a memorial to your loved one, moved, removed or altered may make you feel very much unwelcome in a space. Marginalisation may result from the deliberate absence of a cherished physical symbol, as much as from the presence of a contested one.

To return to the goal of what I have termed 'co-memoration', would the removal of physical symbols of this nature actually help people in Northern Ireland to remember *together*? Might it not result in people remembering separately, recollecting opposing narratives, whilst sharing the same physical space? True, that such a space might no longer have the effect of reinforcing or siding with one of these opposing narratives could be deemed an improvement. Yet, if commemoration which is truly co-memoration must demonstrate and promote reconciliation, then surely worship spaces must somehow contest the tendency to remember separately in each other's presence. Is there an alternative, which reflects a diversity of allegiances and loyalties under the greater allegiance and loyalty to the cause of Christ? An alternative which neither privileges a particular set of narratives, thus rendering commemoration exclusive, nor refuses embodied narrative altogether, thus rendering commemoration incongruous as remembrances in a place which admits no markers of its past?

Verbal Narratives: The Liturgy

Should a way forward to worship spaces which promote co-memoration be found, then even such progress may well be made in vain, if the verbal narratives of the liturgy escape critical attention. For there would remain the question of how an inclusive language of commemoration is to be arrived at. As with physical symbols, the task which this chapter aims at is to identify the probable obstacles in the path to remembering together. In attempting to do so, I will limit myself here to a discussion of the problems posed by one of the most widely used verses of Scripture in Remembrance Sunday liturgies.

The Use of John 15:13

John 15:13, 'Greater love has no one than this that they lie down their life for their friends' (NIVUK), is, certainly, prevalent among the biblical texts chosen for commemoration services in this context. There is a difficulty, however, where this text is offered in such a way as to imply a parallel between Christ's sacrifice on the cross and the contribution to society of those being remembered, either in what is said or left unsaid by way of interpretation. This use of the text is problematic on several counts, not least, because of the distance between conflict-related deaths and the apparent meaning of these words in the context of the Gospel account. There is not only distance but also difference here. That is to say, the difference between the sacrifice made by Christ on the cross and the sacrifice of those who died or suffered in the course of a conflict is not only a quantitative question of magnitude, but a qualitative one of irreducible differences.

The presence of such qualitative differences becomes evident with a comparison between Christ's death and the deaths of those who might be considered combatants and non-combatants in conflict. On the one hand, Christ's death differs from that of a combatant in that he offered no violence, even as a means of self-defence. On the other hand, his death remains distinct from that of most non-combatants in that it was an act of wilful and necessary sacrifice, rather than unfortunate tragedy. This does not make a particularly convincing case for drawing a strong parallel.

What is to be done with John 15:13 then? Might it be retained in Remembrance Sunday liturgies in spite of these objections? Can an alternative interpretation of its relevance to the commemoration of conflict be offered which recognises the distance and difference involved? Can the deaths and casualties of combatants and non-combatants be distanced from the nature of the death of the crucified, while at the same time maintaining the immense value of their lives, the value of the friends Christ laid down his life for? Such an alternative explanation must be offered, for even if a parallel is not drawn (even if the preaching is based on a different text), if its use in the liturgy is retained, there would at least appear to be an invitation to interpret its relevance in this way, not least through habit.

In addition to the exegetical liberties required, there is a further reason, specific to this context and many like it, why this type of parallel should be avoided. Drawing such parallels in conflict and post-conflict societies implies the taking of a position on what constitutes legitimate violence. Jesus' refusal to offer violent resistance in the face of his suffering can only be dismissed as unobtrusive to the drawing of a parallel with the deaths of combatants, by allowing the possibility that some violence can be considered morally legitimate. Actually, going on to draw a parallel with the deaths of a specific group of combatants in a conflict then implies that the physical force they may have used constituted legitimate violence. In the context of commemorating international conflicts this is not usually a major issue, that is to say in contexts where it is generally accepted that a 'war' was being fought by combatants.[22] In the context of the conflict in Northern Ireland however, this is a deeply contested issue.

The extension of the sacrificial language of John 15:13 to describe the death of combatants, requires a consensus about legitimate violence. Surely, those remembering together must agree on who is to be remembered as laying down their life for their friends as Jesus did, and who was involved in criminality? Doing so, would require a level of agreement about what, and whose, violence was legitimate, about what was combat, and who were combatants, as opposed to criminal activity and criminal actors, which does not currently exist across the current context. When such parallels are drawn in a service of commemoration then, they necessarily imply a particular stance on legitimate violence, and that stance has the potential to include and exclude from the act of remembrance taking place. A service of commemoration which includes the drawing of such a parallel seems destined to fall short of facilitating an inclusive act of co-memoration. For, if it were to adopt the extreme position that all of those employing violent means in the conflict did so legitimately, then it would alienate the many who believed such a position to be intolerable. The desire to honour the memory of those known and unknown to the worshipping community, by placing their service in proximity to the ultimate sacrifice made by Christ is understandable. However, it can only be maintained through questionable exegesis and at the expense of inclusivity.

In spite of this, John 15:13 may still have a place in liturgies of remembrance in this context. Viewed in light of the preceding verse's command

---

[22] The exception, of course, is in specific cases where deviation from the conventions governing the conduct of international warfare is considered to have occurred.

to 'love one another as I have loved you', Verse 13's laying down of life for friends comes in the context of a redefinition of 'friends'. This definition of 'friends', has radically reconciliatory implications. The love that Christ calls his disciples to show to one another is a love that transcends localised loyalties and divisions wrought by past conflicts. He has laid down his life for friends who have been at enmity with him and with each other. He has given them, not least through the act of laying down his life for them, a bond which challenges the claims of all other bonds on the loyalties of those who follow him. His followers are forced to reconsider the relationship they have with those previously termed 'them' and 'theirs', or to use the vernacular of the context, 'the other side', in light of what it means to be together 'His'. It is a text then which has the potential to illustrate how fraught with difficulty commemorating conflict can be, but which can also be interpreted as a call to face those difficulties.

CONCLUSION

A Way Forward

The use of John 15 suggested here has the potential to bring about co-memoration of a common identity in, and allegiance to, Christ. To reconsider what it means to remember conflict together in light of this remembrance, is to do public theology as Moltmann understands it, by 'thinking about what is of general concern in the light of hope in Christ for the kingdom of God'.[23] It is in light of the common identity as 'friends' in, and of, Christ, and the loyalty to Him and His Kingdom, that Christian theologians and churches must reflect on the presence of commemorative symbols in Chritian worship spaces and their approach to remembrance liturgies. Surely, it is by prioritising this identity, and this loyalty, that a way forward to more inclusive co-memoration will be found.

In searching for that way forward, this chapter underlines the need for further research to be done on this subject within the field of public theology. It also suggests the shape of that future research by demonstrating the relevance of post-colonial methods to this task. Where such research strives at a better understanding of the commemorative potentials and pitfalls within Protestant worship communities, it must engage with those from nationalist and republican backgrounds who have, in various ways,

---

[23] Moltmann, God for a Secular Society, p. 1.

found themselves part of these communities. Where they have found themselves on the margins of these communities as a result of an alienating experience of commemoration, these experiences cannot be ignored. The outlining of areas of difficulty here, in the physical symbols (flags, emblems and memorials) and in liturgical approaches to remembrance, is offered as a framework to bring focus to such future engagement.

BIBLIOGRAPHY

Ignatieff, Michael. 1997. *The Warrior's Honor: Ethnic War and the Modern Conscience*. New York: Henry Holt.

McGrath, F.C. 2012. Settler Nationalism: Ulster Unionism and Postcolonial Theory. *Irish Studies Review* 20: 463–485.

Moltmann, Jürgen. 1999. *God for a Secular Society*. In *The Public Relevance of Theology*. London: SCM Press.

Wilson, Robin. September 2016. *Northern Ireland Peace Monitoring Report, Number Four*. Northern Ireland Community Relations Council.

ADDITIONAL REFERENCES

Albion News. 2015. *The Official West Bromwich Albion Matchday Programme*.

BBC News Northern Ireland. 2015, October 22. *Minister Resigns After Removing British Legion Flags*. http://www.bbc.co.uk/news/uk-northern-ireland-34604227. Accessed 23 August 2017.

Madmen Season 4 Episode 5. 2010. *The Chrysanthemum and the Sword*. AMC.

The Holy Bible. 1984. *New International Version*. London: Hodder & Stoughton.

The Report of the Bloody Sunday Inquiry. 2010. London: The Stationery Office.

CHAPTER 5

A Postcolonial Ethnographic Reading of Migrant/Refugee Faith Communities in Bengaluru

C. I. David Joy

INTRODUCTION

A postcolonial world view is required to locate the struggles and pains of the ordinary people who have no access to power structures and hierarchical status of the society. However, linking postcolonial reading strategy with ethnographic studies today is a very challenging one as it demands the bringing together of many disciplines and faculties critically and analytically. This chapter is an attempt to define postcolonial ethnography with the help of three case studies in relation to the pathos of the migrants and refugees from villages and sub-urbans into Bangalore, a metropolitan city. Since my interest is to look at the faith dimension of the issue, I will discuss how their faith formulations happened in the encountering locale.

C. I. David Joy (✉)
United Theological College, Bangalore, Karnataka, India

© The Author(s) 2019
J. Dunn et al. (eds.), *Multiple Faiths in Postcolonial Cities*, Postcolonialism and Religions,
https://doi.org/10.1007/978-3-030-17144-5_5

ETHNOGRAPHY

While talking about ethnographic reading, it is important to note the scope and limitations of such a reading. It has been successfully applied in the field of sociology and anthropology by researchers to bring out the basic features of a society/community. However, it is carefully noted that there are no pioneer studies linking both postcolonialism and ethnography to locate the foundational elements of the status of a floating community of any metropolitan framework. I name it floating because of its flexible identity and nature.

Mark Galliford's study *Voicing a Postcolonial Ethnography* is an excellent example of how a postcolonial view point could help developing ethnography, whether par-ethnography or incidental ethnography of a community.[1] It is significant as the community is not free from colonial inheritance and internal colonialism due to various institutions in the country. Devika Chawla's paper "Can There Be a Postcolonial Ethnography?" *raises a very significant question about the identity of the speaker and audience as postcolonial ethnography refers to such realms.*[2] Since colonialism altered or reshaped cultures in India, ethnography is key in estimating the cultural dynamics of a community. It is noted that ethnography is a clear analysis of cultures of all types including their undercurrents. While discussing the communities which were forced to migrate into the cities due to socio-cultural reasons, it is important to estimate the dimensions of colonial influence encountered by them. When I say colonial influence, I am not limiting this term to the political realm alone, but extending it to socio-cultural and religious realms. Ethnographic studies in the field are challenging affairs, as the features and components of the society emerged during the colonial period. The systems that continue to dominate and design affairs seem to be complex and hegemonic in the nature of the exploitation their colonial political origin. Therefore, applying ethnographic studies in the field must be done carefully and analytically. Simone Krunger explains ethnography after a systematic study. She claims that ethnographers explore human behaviour, construction of the social order and culture of the people. The greatest benefit of doing ethnography is that it can

---

[1] Mark Galliford, *Voicing a Postcolonial Ethnography*, Canberra, National Museum Press, 2002.

[2] Devika Chawla, "Can There Be a Postcolonial Ethnography?" Paper presented at the annual meeting of the NCA 96th Annual Convention, Hilton San Francisco, San Francisco, CA.

read things from within the society by taking a naturalistic setting of the society. Since ethnography will lead to the formation of theories and patterns of reading, it is important to read it from the postcolonial theoretical point of view for a postcolonial world.

I consider a postcolonial ethnographic reading to be more fruitful and meaningful than any other reading strategies as I deal with case studies of refugees and their faith formations. D. Soyini Madison's 2012 book *Critical Ethnography: Method, Ethics, and Performance* is a welcome addition to the field.[3] After a careful analysis of the case and context, it is important "to address processes of unfairness or injustice within a particular lived domain" which is called critical ethnography.[4] It is noted that a researcher should have a personal engagement in doing ethnographic studies as ethnography reveals the hidden dimensions of a life situation of a community. While addressing the issues of refugees and migrants and their faith issues, I have felt a critical engagement; hence I term the method as ethnography. In the same way J.J. Roy Burman's 2010 book *Ethnography of a Denotified Tribe* is an important contribution to the field of cultural ethnography as it describes how and why the identity formation of a particular community emerged with the help of socio-political and religio-cultural elements of a community. Roy Burman argues:

> Cultural anthropology and social anthropology were developed around ethnographic research and their canonical texts are mostly ethnographies. Ethnography mainly refers to field based study. It provides an amount of a particular culture, society or community. The field work usually involves spending a year or more in another society, living with the local people and learning about their ways of life. Ethnographers are participant observers. They take part in events they study because it helps with understanding local behaviour and thought.[5]

Therefore, my observations about the refugees and migrants and their postcolonial milieu could be explained and justified by using postcolonial ethnographic reading as ethnographic studies involve long-term observations and engagements. Since the social phenomenon of a community is

---

[3] D. Soyini Madison, *Critical Ethnography: Method, Ethics, and Performance*, London, Sage Publications, 2012.

[4] Ibid., 5.

[5] J.J. Roy Burman, *Ethnography of a Denotified Tribe*, New Delhi, Mittal Publications, 2010, 3.

unique it requires a careful treatment and analysis. Here I consider the importance of ethnography as it brings forth the mind of the community through observation and analysis of data. It is said about the legitimate role of an ethnographer, "even when the ethnographer is acting as observer, he or she may be an important audience for the participants".[6]

POSTCOLONIAL READING

Since I am a practitioner of postcolonial hermeneutics, specifically in the Christian religion and scripture, I try to understand the postcolonial framework from a Christian hermeneutical view point. A relevant postcolonial reading here should be the one that takes the multiple layers of culture in a particular context. Therefore, I suggest that more insights in terms of understanding culture should be used to perceive things in a postcolonial manner. In order to justify the use of postcolonial framework for estimating the milieu of refugees and migrants and their faith affinities, I explain postcolonial hermeneutics as I have been using them to engage with the biblical texts within my context. R.S. Sugirtharajah in a brilliant and influential 2007 article, "Tsunami, Text and Trauma: Hermeneutics After the Asian Tsunami", explains "the hermeneutical enterprise seems to be an easier exercise in calmer and more comfortable times".[7] Unlike the well-established Western academy, Indian New Testament scholars and researchers have to boldly and theologically evaluate many such scenarios, as very often crises and encounters enter into church and academy. One should not, or cannot, run away from such scenes, but has to address the issues with the help of the Bible and faith imagination. Thus the faith issues of refugees and migrants in a postcolonial metropolitan city, namely Bengaluru, become the focus of my analysis here.

It is time for New Testament researchers to talk about a "post-literary, post-theoretical and post-methodological" phase of research as the socio-political and religio-cultural maps shift from one dimension to the other rapidly.[8] A specific reason behind such a trajectory is the use of insights from poststructuralism, postcolonial theory, cultural studies, queer theory

---

[6] Martin Hammersley and Paul Atkinson, *Ethnography: Principles in Practice*, London, Routledge, 1995, 222.

[7] R.S. Sugirtharajah, "Tsunami, Text and Trauma: Hermeneutics After the Asian Tsunami" in *Biblical Interpretation* 15, 2007, 134.

[8] Stephen D. Moore, "A Modest Manifesto for New Testament Literary Criticism: How to Interface with a Literary Studies Field That Is Post-Literary, Post-Theoretical and Post-Methodological", in *Biblical Interpretation* 15, 2007, 1.

and masculinity studies, and economic analysis in the research and study of New Testament.[9] How does a post-theoretical phase emerge? If a theory or method is being institutionalized or dominated by those who belong to the dominant and hegemonic class, researchers at the margins or periphery may be forced to think of a post-theoretical phase. For instance, the much celebrated literary criticism "assimilate[s] most smoothly with traditional historical criticism".[10] It is always said by New Testament researchers that the research seems to be traditional and conventional, and a simple reason for this is the failure of the researcher to define and identify the interface between New Testament studies and current literary and political studies. Stephen D. Moore observes:

> Biblical studies too, of course, although certainly in a less concerned fashion than literary studies, has increasingly veered into the "political" in recent decades. I would venture to say, however, the literary studies has provided little direct impetus for this swerve in biblical studies. Notable political developments in literary studies such as new historicism, postcolonial studies, and queer studies, have only been taken up in biblical studies in the past decade or less and remain on the fringes of the field.[11]

Moore's observations are forward looking and offer new directions in terms of research and studies on historicity attached to the sources of New Testament. It is noted that Jesus' personality has been analysed and presented to be "the synthesis of both Galilean peasant and urban Greek sophisticate".[12] Siker argues that in the ongoing project of the Historical Jesus, there is a "role of white privilege" and other kinds of constructions are sidelined by dominant institutions of biblical studies. It is reflected even in some publications and other forums where current New Testament debates are taking place. Some arguments are indeed interesting as some claim "not only are they like [Jesus], Jesus is like them".[13] It is a very good spring board for arriving at certain valuable conclusions about the faith issues of refugees and migrants in a postcolonial metropolitan city, namely Bengaluru. Tim Woods' 2011 book *Beginning Postmodernism* presents "a

[9] Ibid.

[10] Ibid., 5.

[11] Ibid., 7.

[12] Jeffrey S. Siker, "Historicizing a Racialized Jesus: Case Studies in the "Black Christ," the "Mestizo Christ," and White Critique", in *Bible Interpretation* 15, 2007, 26.

[13] Ibid., 27.

sense of the potential for ideological interrogation" to address the issues of faith communities in a postmodern context.[14]

Postcolonialism has been accepted as a possible reading strategy to locate the voice and space of the people of the margins in most of the countries that bear the marks of colonialism. Couze Venn's 2006 book *The Postcolonial Challenge: Towards Alternative Worlds* is an important contribution to the field that suggests postcoloniality is a major feature in the new world order.[15] While describing the scope of postcolonialism, Venn explains:

> It follows that the prefix in postcoloniality is not meant to signal the end of the previous period but to stand for the sign of an emancipator project, that is, it announces a goal yet to be realized: that of dismantling the economic, political and social structures and values, the attitudes and ideas that appeared with European colonialism and its complex combination with capitalism and Western modernity, and it is important to add, with pre-existing forms of exploitation.[16]

Therefore, it is argued that postcolonialism today appears to be a method of reading that accommodates many perspectives and tools of reading. I consider it as a possible alternative reading strategy to estimate the context as it has a powerful dimension of liberation. Thus people of the margins can aspire for a better world order and life situation.

While doing theology and hermeneutics, a major question emerges from the field of ethics as many ethical paradigms in the Christian religion have been shaped within the parameters of New Testament texts. The same question is significant in a postcolonial ethnographic reading of the faith issues of refugees and migrants in a postcolonial metropolitan city, namely Bengaluru. Daniel Patte states:

> Because of the polyvalence of the ethical teaching of each biblical text and because of the propriety of multiple critical interpretations, the critical study of the ethical teaching of New Testament texts must be envisioned as a comparative study aimed at elucidating characteristics of the interpretive process of several interpretations.[17]

---

[14] Tim Woods, *Beginning Postmodernism*, New Delhi, Viva Books, 2011, 234.

[15] Couze Venn, *The Postcolonial Challenge: Towards Alternative Worlds*, London, Sage Publications, 2006.

[16] Ibid., 4.

[17] Daniel Patte, "New Testament Ethics: Envisioning Its Critical Study in This Day and Age", in *Perspectives in Religious Studies* 23, 1996, 183.

The role of New Testament theology in the process of evolving a possible route for a legitimate understanding of the New Testament has been under examination in recent decades. It is said that New Testament theology will enable the reading of the New Testament to clearly elucidate the issues and concerns related to orthodoxy and heresy in the texts.[18] Interestingly, New Testament theology today picks up issues regarding the milieu and community behind every text, by addressing current questions about the theological framework about a text. It is noted that the history of Christianity in the early period should also be brought to the forefront of our debate today. Neil Richardson justifies this argument by pointing out the issues and questions in John's Gospel, specifically highlighting the world and history. He states:

> Under the Roman Empire, they often faced acute moral dilemmas and, until the end of the second century, condemned and refused military service in the Roman Army.[19]

Similar situations created a crisis in the life of early Church in terms of identity and mobility with freedom. Recent studies and researches in the field of New Testament theology have opened up new horizons in understanding the real world of New Testament. Rosi Braidotti, while analysing the present scenario of the New Testament theology, exposes the situation in Matthean scholarship:

> I feel a real urgency to elaborate alternative accounts, to learn to work differently about the subject, to invent new frameworks, new images, new modes of thought. Women's power as depicted in the gospel story consists in giving birth, following Jesus, hearing his teaching, being fed with the crowds, claiming healing, entering into debate in a way that changed Jesus' perspective on his ministry, exercising diakonia, remaining faithful at the site of Jesus' death, faithfully visiting his place of burial, encountering the risen Jesus, and going off to proclaim that Jesus had indeed been raised from the dead.[20]

---

[18] Neil Richardson, *John for Today: Reading the Fourth Gospel*, London, SCM Press, 2010, 133.

[19] Ibid., 62.

[20] Elaine M. Wainwright, *Shall We Look for Another? A Feminist Rereading of the Matthean Jesus*, Maryknoll, Orbis, 1998, 48.

Women disciples of Jesus and their participation in the ministry and mission of Jesus have always been a major question for debate in the study of the New Testament. It is noted that feminist perspectives and readings opened up a new area for debate by placing the role of women in the Jesus movement. If this pattern is followed, there could be innovative interpretations in the study of the New Testament. Sean Freyne, in a brilliant analysis of the Galilean milieu of the gospel, argues:

> The situation envisaged in this scenario represents a rather different stage in the social transformation of Galilee to that which in our account Jesus encountered in the twenties. We have maintained that Jesus' message was addressed both to land owing peasants (the majority of the population of lower Galilee) and the lower levels of the retain class.[21]

What impact could this view offer to New Testament theology is an important question to be addressed. Sean Freyne clearly differs with John Dominic Crossan and others in analysing the milieu of Jesus. New Testament study today might offer new guidelines for doing theology as the study seems to be inter-disciplinary by all means in terms of emerging new paradigms for understanding. Such inter-disciplinary approaches will definitely have an impact on deriving and defining a relevant theology.

CASE STUDIES

A Migrant from Trivandrum

Gabriel was a migrant from Trivandrum to Bengaluru in the 1980s due to unemployment and poverty. He came to Bengaluru with his wife and four children. He was a Protestant Christian, however, for various reasons he had to join the local Catholic church. He was doing some business selling lunch packets near a Catholic school. In order to get the support of the local church, he and his family joined the Catholic church. But he maintained their membership with the Protestant church in Trivandrum. When asked he told me that he was a refugee in Bengaluru and had some recognition in Trivandrum. After 30 years of life, he was feeling insecure in Bengaluru. Applying postcolonial ethnography, in order to analyse the life

---

[21] Sean Freyne, *Galilee and Gospel*, Leiden, Brill, 2002, 228.

situation of Gabriel is a challenging task as it involves the process of writing the history of two sociological contexts.

While some local Protestant Christian groups tried to support Gabriel, this was unsuccessful. Gabriel was looking for a space which could enable him to define his identity.

A Tibetan Refugee

Jimpa was forced to come to Bengaluru to work in a local beauty parlour. She wanted to join the Tibetan community in Mysuru, but her employer did not permit her. She felt that only with her own community and people could she define her identity, as identity is inter-connected with culture. In Bengaluru there are strong Tibetan support groups which organize regular cultural and religious programmes showing solidarity with the people on the edges, specifically the Tibetan refugees. At the same time, many Tibetans express that only through defining their identity in geopolitical terms may they achieve their goal. In my opinion, inter-religious groups can do wonders in terms of offering solidarity to the refugees in a postcolonial context.

A Bihari Worker

Baburana left Bihar after a famine in his village. He joined a local hotel in Vasanth Nagar as a member of the maintenance staff. He was working almost 18 hours to satisfy the owner of the hotel. He wanted to go back to his village in Bihar to live with dignity. Such exploitations are part of colonial rule in many parts of India and neo-colonial forces shamelessly continue the practice. It is important to bring forth postcolonial reading strategies to understand the level of exploitation in the cities. Baburana was approached by some of my students as part of their field exposure with the offer of legal assistance and other support. However, he was suspicious of the offer due to religious reasons. In order to gain confidence, it is suggested to have an inter-religious space.

Gabriel, Jimpa and Baburana encounter almost same issues of identity and culture and their faith affiliations could not equip them well. However, the local initiatives of inter-religious spaces that consider the postcolonial framework seriously could address some of the issues.

Identity, Culture and Faith Communities

The faith issues of refugees and migrants in a postcolonial metropolitan city, namely Bengaluru, should be understood by analysing the above-mentioned cases as those cases are indeed ethnographic ones due to my long-term involvement and postcolonial ideological stance. In all these cases, their faith factors fluctuate according to the context, though the basic things remain unaltered. Culture is important here as I consider "culture as a specialist field of study was closely associated with the disciplines of anthropology and sociology".[22] Thus it is noted that Gabriel, Jimpa and Baburana are products of cultural conflicts and their quest for identity can be evaluated only by taking postcolonial contexts into account. Why postcolonial theoretical framework is used in a situation or case studies like these is an important concern to be answered. Since the faith issues of refugees and migrants in a postcolonial metropolitan city, namely Bengaluru (Gabriel, Jimpa and Baburana), had been altered or reshaped due to colonial invasion in many ways, it is legitimate to apply this view point. Neeladri Bhattacharya, in her 2001 essay "Remaking Custom: The Discourse and Practice of Colonial Codification", argues that the colonial regime played a very important role in reshaping customs and practices of the native people. She states:

> Like many ideas and attitudes, this interest in the ancient, the popular and the distant made its way into the colonies. Its journey there was attended by all the twists and turns and paradoxes and contortions that such travels usually entail.[23]

This is an enthralling observation as Bhattacharya creatively expresses the embodying of colonial invasion over culture. There had been recordings and documentation of that era officially. It is difficult to study the then context as "these British ethnographic texts reveal as much, or rather a bit less, about Indian custom".[24] The faith issues of refugees and migrants in a postcolonial metropolitan city, namely Bengaluru, ought to be explored

---

[22] Kamala Ganesh and Usha Thakkar, eds., *Culture and the Making of Identity in Contemporary India*, New Delhi, Sage, 2005, 13.

[23] Neeladri Bhattacharya, "Remaking Custom: The Discourse and Practice of Colonial Codification", in eds., R. Champaka Lakshmi and S. Gopal, *Tradition, Dissent and Ideology: Essays in Honour of Romila Thaper*, Delhi, OUP, 2001, 23.

[24] Ibid.

within the postcolonial theoretical framework as colonialism played a key role in cornering refugees and migrants. Most of the refugees and migrants were forced to do so due to the hegemonic policies of colonial rulers, such as ruining the village economy for the sake of industrialization.

Along with a postcolonial framework, cultural anthropology may also play a significant role in assessing the condition of such people. Thomas Rhys Williams defines cultural anthropology in the following way:

> Cultural anthropology is a way of approaching and beginning to comprehend the complex mosaic of the human experience, through the long history of the existence of culture.[25]

By applying the insights of cultural anthropology, how the identity question of refugees and migrants can be addressed emerges as a significant question. Since religion and faith affinities very strongly define the identity question of faith communities today, including refugees and migrants, it is noted that the harmonious co-existence of human society may be encountered by religious fundamentalism. "Religious fundamentalism … appears to be surprisingly strong and influential as a source of identity" today.[26]

Addressing the issue of identity, especially the identity of refugees and migrants, Couze Venn's definition seems to be important. Venn states:

> Identity as a concept thus always directs attention to the relational aspect of subjectivity.[27] Subjectivity and identity are necessarily inter-related when it is a matter of analyzing conduct and beliefs, obliging one to take account of the following mechanisms and their co-articulated operation: those revealed from the perspective of ideology in accounting for the normative content of specific identities, those that inscribe power effects relating to systematic differences such as gender, and mechanisms relating to the historical and cultural specificity of the process.

Identity is not merely a social construct, but it touches all dimensions of socio-political contexts of a society. In a postcolonial context, applying ethnography is very important to consider the cultural aspects of the community.

[25] Thomas Rhys Williams, *Cultural Anthropology*, New Jersey, Prentice Hall, 1990, xiii.
[26] Manuel Castells, *The Power of Identity*, Oxford, Blackwell Publishers, 1998, 13.
[27] Couze Venn, op. cit., 80.

CONCLUSION

Ethnographic observations from a postcolonial view point clearly expose the life situations of Gabriel, Jimpa and Baburana. Their struggle for identity could have been understood by the society very well if religious aspects and faith aspects were taken seriously. In a metropolitan milieu, a postcolonial reading strategy can be applied effectively with the help of ethnographic studies.

BIBLIOGRAPHY

Bhattacharya, Neeladri. 2001. Remaking Custom: The Discourse and Practice of Colonial Codification. In *Tradition, Dissent and Ideology: Essays in Honour of Romila Thaper*, ed. R. Champaka Lakshmi and S. Gopal. Delhi: OUP.

Castells, Manuel. 1998. *The Power of Identity*. Oxford: Blackwell Publishers.

Chawla, Devika. *Can There Be a Postcolonial Ethnography?* Paper presented at the annual meeting of the NCA 96th Annual Convention, Hilton San Francisco, San Francisco CA.

Freyne, Sean. 2002. *Galilee and Gospel*. Leiden: Brill.

Galliford, Mark. 2002. *Voicing a Postcolonial Ethnography*. Canberra: National Museum Press.

Ganesh, Kamala, and Usha Thakkar, eds. 2005. *Culture and the Making of Identity in Contemporary India*. New Delhi: Sage.

Hammersley, Martin, and Paul Atkinson. 1995. *Ethnography: Principles in Practice*. London: Routledge.

Madison, D. Soyini. 2012. *Critical Ethnography: Method, Ethics, and Performance*. London: Sage Publications.

Moore, Stephen D. 2007. A Modest Manifesto for New Testament Literary Criticism: How to Interface with a Literary Studies Field That Is Post-Literary, Post-Theoretical and Post-Methodological. *Biblical Interpretation* 15.

Patte, Daniel. 1996. New Testament Ethics: Envisioning Its Critical Study in This Day and Age. *Perspectives in Religious Studies* 23.

Richardson, Neil. 2010. *John for Today: Reading the Fourth Gospel*. London: SCM Press.

Roy Burman, J.J. 2010. *Ethnography of a Denotified Tribe*. New Delhi: Mittal Publications.

Siker, Jeffrey S. 2007. Historicizing a Racialized Jesus: Case Studies in the "Black Christ," the "Mestizo Christ," and White Critique. *Bible Interpretation* 15.

Sugirtharajah, R.S. 2007. Tsunami, Text and Trauma: Hermeneutics After the Asian Tsunami. *Biblical Interpretation* 15.

Venn, Couze. 2006. *The Postcolonial Challenge: Towards Alternative Worlds.* London: Sage Publications.

Wainwright, Elaine M. 1998. *Shall We Look for Another? A Feminist Rereading of the Matthean Jesus.* Maryknoll: Orbis.

Williams, Thomas Rhys. 1990. *Cultural Anthropology.* New Jersey: Prentice Hall.

Woods, Tim. 2011. *Beginning Postmodernism.* New Delhi: Viva Books.

CHAPTER 6

Worshipping God in a *Mabati* Church: Bishop Jane Akoth's Leadership in the African Israel Nineveh Church

Heleen Joziasse and Esther Mombo

INTRODUCTION

The leadership of women in the church is a significant area of study in African Christianities. In recent years there has been much progress in, and visibility of, the leadership of women at various levels in the different churches in Kenya. This has been recorded in various publications showing that each denomination—whether mission, instituted, or Pentecostal/

Mabati is Kiswahili for 'iron sheets'. *Mabati* churches are made of iron sheets.

H. Joziasse (✉)
Mara Foundation, The Hague, The Netherlands

Utrecht University, Utrecht, The Netherlands

E. Mombo
International Partnerships and Alumni Relations, St. Paul's University,
Limuru, Kenya
e-mail: emombo@spu.ac.ke

© The Author(s) 2019
J. Dunn et al. (eds.), *Multiple Faiths in Postcolonial Cities*, Postcolonialism and Religions,
https://doi.org/10.1007/978-3-030-17144-5_6

87

Charismatic churches—has its own history, structure and laws determining the role and place of women in leadership.[1] In this chapter we describe and analyze the role and place of Moderator Bishop Jane Akoth in an African independent church, the Africa Israel Nineveh Church (AINC),[2] in terms of marginalized agency. The leadership of Jane Akoth is located in Kayole Central Pastoral Office (CPO) covering the semi-informal settlements of Kayole and Matopeni, in Nairobi, Kenya.[3] By focusing on an individual woman in a specific denomination, the divergent views of the church teachings and the predominant views about the roles of women are brought to light. Moreover, studying a particular woman in her position of leadership reveals the contestation of her leadership in various ways.

For members of the AINC, the city of Nairobi is a place of mixed realities. Amid affluence, exhibited by both older and newer churches, most members of AINC find themselves living on the edges of the city and worshiping in *Mabati* churches,[4] in spaces with little or no infrastructure.

---

[1] Publications on the position of women in the denominational and African Instituted Churches in Kenya are among others: Philomena Njeri Mwaura, "Gender and Power in African Christianity: African Instituted Churches and Pentecostal Churches," in *African Christianity: An African Story*, ed. Ogbu Kalu, vol. 3, Perspectives of Christianity Series 5 (Pretoria: University of Pretoria, 2005), 410–45. Cynthia Hoehler-Fatton, *Women of Fire and Spirit: History, Faith, and Gender in Roho Religion in Western Kenya* (New York: Oxford University Press, 1996). Esther Mombo, "The Ordination of Women in Africa: An Historical Perspective," in *Women and Ordination in the Christian Churches: International Perspectives*, ed. Ian Jones, Kirsty Thorpe, and Janet Wootton (London, New York: T&T Clark, 2008). Isabel Apawo Phiri, Devarakshanam Betty Govinden, and Sarojini Nadar, eds., *Her-Stories: Hidden Histories of Women of Faith in Africa* (Pietermaritzburg: Cluster, 2002). Maggie Madimbo, "Supportive Leadership Behavior Key to Breaking the Glass Ceiling in Religious Communities in Malawi," *The Journal of Pan African Studies* 5, no. 2 (April 2012): 27–42. Jane Wakahiu and Mary Salvaterra, "Sustainable Leadership: Lessons and Implications of a Leadership Development Program for Women Religious in Africa," *The Journal of Pan African Studies* 5, no. 2 (April 2012): 150–68. Damaris Parsitau, "Agents of Gendered Change: Empowerment, Salvation and Gendered Transformation in Urban Kenya," in *Pentecostalism and Development*, ed. Dena Freeman, Non-Governmental Public Action (Palgrave Macmillan UK, 2012), 203–21. Musimbi R.A. Kanyoro, *In Search of a Round Table: Gender, Theology & Church Leadership* (Geneva: WCC Publications, 1997).

[2] The name African Israel Church Nineveh (AICN) is used as well.

[3] Jane Owur Akoth was the first woman appointed as Moderator Bishop in the AINC in 2012. This chapter is written as part of a wider book-project about the AINC in which Jane Akoth is involved as co-editor.

[4] *Mabati* or 'iron sheet' churches are often found in informal settlements. The roof and walls of these churches are built of iron sheets with an earthen floor, without amenities. The *Mabati* churches are either empty or with some simple furniture, especially in the front where there is a slight elevation or platform. In the AINC people call this the pulpit or the *Synagogue*.

Fig. 6.1 Bishop Jane (with drum) leads worship—AINC Chemelil 22-1-2017

It is in this context that Jane Akoth exercises and negotiates leadership (Fig. 6.1).

In this chapter first an introduction is given about the historical context of the African Israel Nineveh Church, highlighting its genesis as an African Instituted Church (AIC). Next, a characterization of churches in an urban setting is given, focused on Nairobi, Kenya. Then the leadership in the AINC and the position of women are discussed, concentrating on worship. This is followed by the narration of the story of Jane Akoth: her reasons for joining the AINC, her theological education and her appointment to Moderator Bishop of AINC. Finally, the leadership of Jane Akoth as moderator and bishop in the city of Nairobi is analyzed and evaluated.

African Instituted Churches (AICs) and the AINC

Kenya is a predominant Christian country, with the mission churches—both Protestant and Roman Catholic—as the main representatives.[5] Apart from the mission churches there is a still growing body of churches, known as African Instituted Churches (AICs).[6] This group of AICs is broadly categorized in three main types[7]: the 'Nationalist' or 'Ethiopian' churches, the 'Spiritual churches'[8] and 'African Pentecostal Churches'.[9] The AINC can be characterized as a Spiritual church.[10] Most of these Spiritual churches broke away from mission-founded churches during the colonial

[5] See results of the census of 2009: 82.5% of the Kenyan population is Christian (47.4 % Protestant, 23.3% Roman Catholic, other 11.8%), 11.1% is Muslim, traditional religionists 1.6%, other religion 2.4%. See: https://www.worldatlas.com/articles/religious-beliefs-in-kenya.html and https://www.knbs.or.ke/category/census-2009-summary-of-results/ Accessed August 24, 2018.

[6] These churches initially were designated African Independent Churches, as they were founded by Africans in response to the ways in which Western forms of Christianity were being established. When in the 1960s the missionary churches became independent, the name African Instituted Churches came into vogue. See about the terminology of the AICs: Afe Adogame and Lizo Jafta, "Zionist, Aladura and Roho: African Instituted Churches," in *African Christianity: An African Story*, ed. Ogbu Kalu, vol. 3, Perspectives of Christianity Series 5 (Pretoria: University of Pretoria, 2005), 310–13.

[7] See the typologies: Allan H. Anderson, "African Initiated (Independent) Churches," in *Religions of the World: A Comprehensive Encyclopedia of Beliefs and Practices*, 2nd Edition [6 Volumes], ed. J. Gordon Melton and Martin Baumann, vol. I (Santa Barbara: ABC-CLIO, 2010), 30–36.

[8] Also referred to as 'Spirit churches' or 'Spirit type churches'. Similar churches elsewhere in Africa are designated Zionist churches (in South Africa), *Aladura* or 'praying churches' (in Nigeria) or 'spirit churches' (in Ghana). These churches arose in Kenya from 1915 till the late 1960s. Mwaura holds that this type of churches is still emerging: See Philomena Mwaura, "A Spirituality of Resistance and Hope: African Instituted Churches' Response to Poverty," in *A New Day: Essays on World Christianity in Honor of Lamin Sanneh*, ed. Akintunde E. Akinade (New York: Peter Lang, 2010), 122.

[9] Sometimes referred to as Neo-Pentecostal Churches (NPCs). These churches are oriented toward international Pentecostalism and 'on the whole, in style, language, theology and structure, these churches look to the North and urban society rather than to African tradition'. See: Mwaura, 122.

[10] Philomena Njeri Mwaura, "The Use of Power in African Instituted Churches," *Wajibu. A Journal of Social and Religious Concern* 14, no. 3 (1999). See the thesis of Peter Wilson Kudoyi, "African Israel Nineveh Church: A Theological and Socio-Historical Analysis" (Thesis, Kenyatta University, 1991), 49, http://ir-library.ku.ac.ke/handle/123456789/4983. Padwick lists the AINC as a 'second generation' Roho church. Timothy John Padwick, "Spirit, Desire and the World: Roho Churches of Western Kenya in the Era of Globalization" (PhD, University of Birmingham, 2003), 7, 89, http://etheses.bham.ac.uk/264/.

days—hence they also frequently used the name 'independent churches'. Some of the reasons for the founding of AICs were the racism in mainline (mission) churches, the negative responses to African culture and world-view, and the missionary paternalism at the time. The characteristics of the African Instituted Churches include a more holistic approach to faith and life, their use and application of the Bible, especially the OT with references to the people of Israel, purity laws and so on, and their identification with the Early Church. Another feature is their positive outlook to African culture and worldview, with, among others, the emphasis on community and the acknowledgment of the spiritual world.

The African Israel Nineveh Church is one of the most prominent and numerically one of the biggest of the older African Instituted Churches in Kenya. It was founded in 1942 by Paul David Zakayo Kivuli (1896–1974), later called High Priest Kivuli I.[11] He was a member of the Pentecostal Assemblies of Canada (PAOC), a church established at Nyang'ori in Western Kenya in 1912. Other missionary groups with a strong presence in that area included the Friends African Mission (Quakers), the Church of God, the Salvation Army and the Roman Catholic Church. Kivuli was a supervisor of the PAOC schools and later liaison leader of the church. In 1932 he had an ecstatic spirit baptism experience. He was blind for 18 days and when he regained sight, he embarked on an evangelistic and healing ministry, which experienced resounding success. Kivuli preached the gospel in a way that responded to the situation of the people in content and expression: He enhanced the practice of public confession and introduced bells and drums in the worship, conducting open air meetings and processions with singing and dancing, using traditional African tunes.

Kivuli faced resistance from the senior leadership of the PAOC and this led to the breakaway and the formation of the independent African Israel

---

[11] Information about the AINC is derived from: African Israel Nineveh Church, "Sheria za African Israel Nineveh Church. Translation John M. Kachili" (Nairobi, August 5, 1993). Frederick B. Welbourn and Bethwell A Ogot, *A Place to Feel at Home: A Study of Two Independent Churches in Western Kenya* (London; Nairobi: Oxford U.P., 1966). Peter Wilson Kudoyi, "African Israel Nineveh Church: A Theological and Socio-Historical Analysis" (Thesis, Kenyatta University, 1991), Marko Kuhn, *Prophetic Christianity in Western Kenya: Political, Cultural and Theological Aspects of African Independent Churches* (Frankfurt am Main, etc.: Peter Lang, 2008). Nyahela Caxton, "The Influence of Luyia Traditional Religious Rituals on Christianity: A Case Study of African Israel Church Nineveh in Vihiga County, Kenya" (University of Nairobi, 2015). Timothy John Padwick, "Spirit, Desire and the World: Roho Churches of Western Kenya in the Era of Globalization" (PhD, University of Birmingham, 2003).

Nineveh Church.[12] According to the regulations of the church the name 'African' connotes the founding of church by an African, in Africa. 'Israel' refers to the people that belong to God and have been chosen. The name 'Nineveh' refers to the people of Nineveh who repented. The followers of Kivuli see the world as Nineveh, a sinful city, where people need to confess their sins and repent.[13] The aim of Kivuli was to empower the people while preaching the gospel in a way applicable to the local people's situation by adopting and embracing the culture.[14] Hence, the theology and practices of the AINC are derived from the Bible and the Early Church, as well as from the African culture. Open confession of sins, ecstatic experiences, spirit possession, healing, prophesies and interpretation of dreams, and processions are some of the characteristics of the faith practiced in the AINC.

After the death of Kivuli in 1974 the leadership was passed on to his wife Mama Rebecca Jumba Kivuli (1902–1988).[15] Her leadership was contested and an Executive Committee was appointed to 'help Mama Rebecca lead the church'.[16] About her leadership her predecessor and grandson John Maresa Kivuli II wrote:

> She was supported mostly by women and youth. Most men disliked her leadership (except for a few) due to African culture. She suffered great humiliation from men who denied women's capability and ability to lead in the African context.
>
> Nevertheless, she was an exception in her own right as High Priestess of the African Israel Church Nineveh from 1974 to 1983.[17]

---

[12] Initially, the name of the church was *Huru Salvation African* (*huru* means 'free'). Although this name ultimately expressed what Kivuli and his followers felt, in the context of colonialism (both religious and political) the name *huru* was problematic. Therefore it was changed to African Israel Church Nineveh.

[13] African Israel Nineveh Church, "Sheria za African Israel Nineveh Church. Translation John M. Kachili," 3.

[14] Archbishop John M. Kivuli II, "The Modernization of an African Independent Church," in *Freedom and Interdependence*, ed. Stan Nussbaum (Nairobi, Kenya: Organization of African Instituted Churches, 1994), 58.

[15] This was due to the fact that Kivuli I didn't have a suitable hereditary successor. The son who was destined and theologically trained developed mental health issues.

[16] Archbishop John M. Kivuli II, "The Modernization of an African Independent Church," 59.

[17] Ibid.

Mama Rebecca, known as 'the mother of faith', is mentioned with great respect by the women of the AINC. She is especially remembered for her healing gifts and her views on keeping the traditional values, promoting modest dressing for women (long skirts, no bra), abstention from sexual intercourse on Thursday and Friday, marriage in the church and women being submissive to men.

It was under the leadership of Kivuli II that the church constitution was revised and the roles of Archbishop and High Priest were combined. While the AINC was founded in the areas of Western Kenya and Nyanza among the Luhya and the Luo, it spread to other parts of Kenya as a result of members seeking employment, particularly in the city of Nairobi. It also expanded to other parts of East Africa, to the USA, Europe and Asia (the Philippines).[18] Hence, the membership in the AINC is no longer exclusively Luhya and Luo, but other ethnic communities are as well represented in the AINC, especially in Nairobi. The membership comprises predominantly, but not exclusively, people of the lower socio-economic strata, and in the cities like Nairobi it mainly comprises laborers and people with small businesses.

CHURCH IN THE CITY

The characteristic of post-colonial physicality is urbanization and the growth of slums. Nairobi is not exceptional. The explosion of cities corresponds with the growth of slums.[19] There are approximately 2.5 million slum dwellers in more than 200 settlements in Nairobi, representing 60% of the Nairobi population, and occupying just 6% of the land.[20] Hence, Nairobi is known as a city of huge contrasts. Economically, it is home to

[18] There are no recent estimations of total numbers of members. Archbishop Kivuli II in an interview in Limuru, on 28 October 2016, estimated the membership worldwide at three million people. Padwick estimated the number of members of the AINC in Kenya, Uganda and Tanzania in 2003 at 178,800. See: Padwick, "Spirit, Desire and the World," 94.

[19] An overview of informal settlements based on the population census of 2009 is given in: Ministry of Lands, Housing, and Urban Development, "Kenya Informal Settlements Improvement Project," 8–17, accessed February 1, 2017.
http://documents.worldbank.org/curated/en/791471468038960520/pdf/RP10590V80AFR00Box385406B00PUBLIC0.pdf.

[20] See http://www.kibera.org.uk/facts-info/, http://aphrc.org/wp-content/uploads/2014/08/NCSS2-FINALReport.pdf. See also: African Population and Health Research Center (APHRC), "Population and Health Dynamics in Nairobi's Informal Settlements: Report

the rich and affluent, as well as to the poor and the marginalized. Socio-culturally, the city shows a variety and mixture of both urban and rural characteristics. Many people from rural areas are attracted to this city because of the promise of economic and social upward mobility. Spiritually, the city contains numerous different manifestations in terms of spaces and ways of worship. Most Mission churches and some of the modern Charismatic and Pentecostal churches are located in the central business district of Nairobi, as well as in other areas with well-endowed infrastructure, good buildings and all the social amenities. However, because of the colonial demarcations of the city, most of the African Instituted Churches (AICs) are located in the margins of the city in informal settlements. This also applies to the African Israel Nineveh Church (AINC). In Nairobi the AINC comprises 16 Central Pastoral Offices (CPOs), each organizing a number of assemblies and local congregations. These congregations are situated near or in slum areas as shown in the map (Fig. 6.2).[21]

The informal settlements are overcrowded areas with houses with *mabati roofs*, little or no infrastructure, inadequate access to clean water, poor sanitation and insecurity of tenure. These informal settlements are situated next to posh neighborhoods, near rivers that overflow or in swampy places where people dump their rubbish. 'If natural hazards are magnified by urban poverty, new and entirely artificial hazards are created by poverty's interactions with toxic industries, anarchic traffic and collapsing infrastructure'.[22] Although some scholars observe that in the slums there are more churches than toilets, in many studies on slum areas the role of religion is not included.[23] Robert Neuwirth, however, writes in his book *Shadow Cities. A Billion Squatters. A New Urban World* about the largest slum in Nairobi: 'Sunday in Kibera is for Mungu—for God'.[24]

of the Nairobi Cross-Sectional Slums Survey (NCSS)" (Nairobi: APHRC, 2012), http://aphrc.org/wp-content/uploads/2014/08/NCSS2-FINAL-Report.pdf.

[21] The Assemblies of the AINC in Nairobi are located in Mathare, Ngei, Kariobangi, Korokocho, Kayole, Matopeni, Imara Daima, Riverside, Jerusalem, Kiambiu, Maringo, Langata, Ongata Rongai, Satelite, Kenyatta, Siranga (in Kibera).

[22] Mike Davis, *Planet of Slums* (London, New York: Verso, 2006), 22.

[23] See Esther Mombo, "Religion and Materiality: The Case of Poverty Alleviation," in *Religion and Poverty: PanAfrican Perspectives*, ed. Peter J. Paris (Durham and London: Duke University Press, 2009), 216.

[24] Robert Neuwirth, *Shadow Cities: A Billion Squatters, A New Urban World* (New York: Routledge, 2005), 89. 'Kibera is an old-style shantytown, still made from mud. The city's newer shantytowns are made from corrugated steel sheets set into thin concrete foundations. These communities—Mukuru, Kwa Reuben, Sinai, Kwa Njenga, Gitare Marigu, and scores

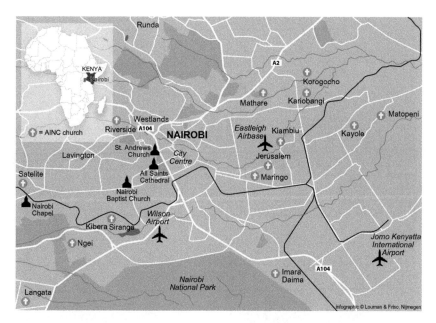

Fig. 6.2 Map of Nairobi. Infographic ©Louman & Friso, Nijmegen. Used with permission

In the mud walled chapels of Pentecostal Assemblies of God, people clap and shout and speak in tongues. At the Catholic Church Mexican priests celebrate mass in Kiswahili while a choir voices hymns with the accompaniment of a melodica and some traditional drums. The Salvation Army parades through the community to the beat of tambourines, looking for errant souls.[25]

In his vivid description of the spiritual life in this informal settlement, a procession of members of the AINC as shown in the figures, could have been rightly included (Fig. 6.3).

Others emphasize not the spiritual impact on peoples' lives but the material gain which these churches in the slums (supposedly) aim at: 'A

---

of others follow the Nairobi and Ngong rivers as they run south and east from town, stretching for miles along the edge of the city's industrial area, through abandoned rock quarries, past the massive garbage dump and stretching on towards the international airport'. Ibid., 72.

[25] Neuwirth, *Shadow Cities*, 89.

Fig. 6.3 Procession Buruburu 22 July 2018

church is a good business … Once you get the people in, you can take a collection'.[13] This appears one of the motivating factors for starting churches in the slums.

LEADERSHIP IN THE AINC

The leadership styles of the AINC developed around the founder Kivuli I; his charisma and skills initially shaped the structures of the church. The organization of the church has been gradually adjusted in the different periods to meet the socio-religious, economic and political needs of the members, as well as to meet the growth in numbers and geographical expansion of the church. The different organizational structures and titles of leaders seem to be a blend, composed from the different denominational practices of the surrounding churches by that time: the Quakers, the Salvation Army, Pentecostals, the Anglican Church, Church of God and so on. The Luhya religious worldview on leadership has also impacted structures of the AINC.

The church organization comprises 16 administrative departments that take care of both the spiritual and physical needs of the members, for example, the gender department, led by women and taking care of the roles ascribed to women, the department for development and infrastructure, the health department, the youth department.[26] The church has a separate department, *Mama Mima*, for economic empowerment of women.[27]

The leadership structure of the church includes offices which incorporate both the spiritual and administrative dimensions, hence the use of double titles. The Archbishop/High Priest operates on an international level as the leader of the AINC. The High Priest appoints (senior and junior) Priests and Priestesses, who are spiritual officers in the churches in the different nations and regions. The Priests and Priestesses are entitled to pray, preach, anoint people, initiate marriage and so on. (Fig. 6.4).

The High Priest appoints the Bishops who lead the AINC in the various countries. He also ordains the Moderator Bishops in the Central Pastoral Offices, of which Jane Akoth is one. Bishops are both administrative and spiritual leaders.[28] Under the Moderator Bishops reside the Pastors who are in charge of an Assembly or a Pastorate. In an Assembly reside all congregations with a Friday service in a given geographical area. The roles of the Pastor include conducting a name-giving ceremony to a newborn baby on the eighth day, praying for the sick and visiting the homes of the church members to pray for 'good health and prosperity both spiritual and physical'.[29] Under the Pastors work the local church elders who run the day-to-day affairs of a congregation. He/she, for instance, arranges assistance for members who are in need and intervenes in domestic problems. He/she also visits and prays for sick members of the congregation and for people outside the church. All leaders are supposed to be knowledgeable and should be in a position to instruct others in the church and newcomers.

---

[26] Caxton in her thesis describes the initial organization of the AINC as being structured around Departments: Caxton, "The Influence of Luyia Traditional Religious Rituals on Christianity: A Case Study of African Israel Church Nineveh in Vihiga County, Kenya," 118–20. In 2017 there were 16 different Departments.

[27] See African Israel Nineveh Church, "Sheria za African Israel Nineveh Church. Translation John M. Kachili," 22–24. Women are the majority in the church and are expected to provide for the material welfare of the church and of their families. While economic empowerment is strongly emphasized the attitude toward material wellbeing is ambivalent. Money is important as far as the daily needs are concerned, but it is not for hoarding, as for AINC-members, richness is primarily sought in heaven and not on earth.

[28] Ibid., 7–9.

[29] Kudoyi, "African Israel Nineveh Church," 78.

Fig. 6.4   Priestess in Buruburu energizing the procession, 22-7-2018

DIFFERENT VOICES CONCERNING THE LEADERSHIP OF WOMEN

According to the church regulations all leadership is from God and any qualified person can be a leader by the power of God, whether a man, a woman or youth.[30] At the same time all leadership positions in the AINC are shared in co-leadership:

> from Sunday 9th 1993, a man will lead together with the wife in any given church post. (…) No husband will be prayed for leadership without the permission of the wife and vice versa. (…) If the couples are not married officially in the church they are not allowed in leadership. Unmarried and widows who are ready to serve the church will take a vow by faith just like others.[31]

---

[30] African Israel Nineveh Church, "Sheria za African Israel Nineveh Church. Translation John M. Kachili," 4.

[31] Ibid., 27–28.

Hence, when a man is ordained as Bishop, his wife is ordained as co-Bishop and vice versa, and this co-leadership is practiced on all levels in the church.[32] Yet, the leadership styles in the AINC seem to be dynamic and influenced by societal realities.[33] While this provision of co-leadership appears to enhance availability/openness of leadership to both genders, the reality is complex and challenging especially when the partners don't belong to the same church or when one is not a Christian.

A major challenge to women's leadership are the different voices in the AINC reflected in the Sheria za AINC (the church regulations) on the role and position of women. Historically the position of women in leadership in the AINC was secondary to that of men. Peter Kudoyi, for instance, recalls the study of Sangree, conducted in 1956, who describes the organization of the AINC as being modeled after the Friends Church in Kenya and parallel to that of the traditional Abaluhyia social and religious organization, where women had secondary authority positions except where leading of women and children was involved.[34] Between 1942 and 1983 the offices of women in the AINC included taking care of the evangelists' accommodation and food, washing their clothes, giving testimonies (or preaching) in crusades, singing, teaching women on family issues and church doctrines, bringing peace in family with conflicts, cleaning the church, carrying children to the pastor for dedication and leading of women in fellowships.[35] Simultaneously and from the onset of the church, women did perform roles as priestesses, depending on gifts of the spirit, and women had a role in dreaming and interpreting dreams and prophesying as well as in healing.

It was in 1983 that the High Priest Kivuli II introduced a new constitution in which the roles of women were redefined. Women were allowed to

[32] It is in rare occasions that single people are appointed to leadership positions. Those who are widowed can remain in office, especially widows depending on the age and the skills they have. Widows may be appointed to the position of the late husband. This, however, is not a common practice.

[33] This flexibility in co-leadership is spelled out in the legislation of the church: 'They will work together and recognized equally by the church. They are the ones to determine how they will work without any friction or collision and without shame before the congregants'. African Israel Nineveh Church, "Sheria za African Israel Nineveh Church. Translation John M. Kachili," 28.

[34] Kudoyi, "African Israel Nineveh Church," 18.

[35] Jane Akoth, *Role of Women in African Israel Nineveh Church from 1942–2009. A historical analysis of the role of women leaders, challenges and opportunities in ministry.* Research Paper, SPU 2010, 19.

lead equally with men, to dedicate newborn babies, to baptize both adults and children, to sing, to preach in the pulpit, to lead processions and to conduct burial services.[36] However, women endowed with leadership positions are still challenged by the cultural and biblical views (esp. from Proverbs and Ezra) on the roles of women in church and society.[37] Besides equality in leadership roles, the Sheria za AINC defines the roles of women in terms of welcoming visitors (providing food, accommodation and transport fare); being quiet, disciplined and knowledgeable; being supportive and nurturing to the leaders of the church; responsible for the cleanliness and health of the church and the family; being industrious and through business uplifting the church and the family. Overall, the position of a woman is defined as someone who supports and respects (the authority of) her husband.[38]

The implication is that in practice women leaders struggle to officiate the roles of blessing, conducting marriages and ordination, because cultural roles and expectation prevent them from actually performing these leadership roles.[39] The dominant view is that a man can't be blessed by a woman and that women lack education and hence can't register an official marriage. Biblical interpretations on the headship of men engrave these views and prevent women from performing these leadership roles.

Women in leadership positions in the AINC seem to be continually negotiating between the cultural and biblical gender roles ascribed to them as women and the officially advocated roles for leaders by the church. Both realities are described and advocated for in the church regulations, creating conflicting expectations.

Worship and the 'Walk of Witness'

Worship within the AINC has a very specific and prominent place. The worshippers of the AINC are recognized through uniformity of dressing, wearing white robes and caps/scarves with red embroidered inscriptions

[36] All the above-mentioned offices are strictly forbidden for women when they have their period.

[37] African Israel Nineveh Church, "Sheria za African Israel Nineveh Church" (Nairobi, August 5, 1993. Transl. J.M. Kachili), 8, 19–20.

[38] African Israel Nineveh Church, "Sheria za African Israel Nineveh Church," 17, 19.

[39] See Akoth, 'Role of Women in African Israel Nineveh Church', 20.

with the name of the church.[40] The basic tenets of worship in the AINC include prayers, oral confession of sin and exorcism, singing accompanied by drumming, ringing of bells and dancing, reading the Bible, offering, preaching, sharing and interpretation of dreams.

The AINC keeps two days of worship. The Friday is the 'Sabbath Day', a day of confession in remembrance of Good Friday, which is reenacted every week throughout the year. This Friday worship is preceded by spiritual and physical preparation on Thursday, for instance, by not eating meat and abstaining from sexual intercourse. Menstruation is regarded as a state of uncleanliness, hence women in their menses can't join the worship, nor are they allowed to touch 'holy objects' at home, for example, the Bible and church clothes. On Friday there is a set (but not written) liturgy from 9:00 to 15:00 with songs, confessions, readings referring to the crucifixion of Jesus, preaching and blessings.[41] On Sunday there is an open air meeting and a procession leading along markets, streets and roads toward the church (Fig. 6.5).

The procession is both an act of worship and a walk of witness. The members march in three lines and sing short phrases, accompanied by drums and bells, while two men carry a flag.[42] In the one-line repetitive choruses, people are invited to join the procession and to come to church. They sing, for instance: 'Come to church and you will be saved', 'Repent before time', and 'Jesus is coming'. After having gone around the church three times, the members of the congregation remove their shoes before they enter the church.[43] Then the door(s) are closed and the worship in the church starts. Since in Nairobi most of the members of the AINC are engaged in economic activities on Friday, the Sabbath is transferred to Sunday and preceded by the procession. The Moderator Bishop takes the lead in these processions, making sure that the lines are closed, the pace is

[40] The wearing of white robes and caps/headscarves by all members (both young and old) with the signs A. Israel N. on the chest and front part of the caps and scarves expresses the unity of the members.

[41] The service is opened by singing three songs and simultaneously confession of sins, followed by prayers? And exorcism (kush, kush), greetings of visitors, announcement of leaders, collection, handing over to the leaders in the pulpit, readings from Bible and sermon, song and blessings.

[42] The colors of the flag are green, white and red, symbolizing the fertile African land, the blood of Jesus and the forgiveness of sins of all people. The white is above gender, race, class and age.

[43] This is required only in the rural areas, not in Nairobi.

Fig. 6.5 Procession in three lines, Buruburu 22-7-2018

kept, the songs are sung and people in trance are guided. It is against this background that we analyze the leadership of Moderator Bishop Jane Akoth.

THE MODERATOR BISHOP JANE AKOTH

Jane Akoth Owur was born and brought up in difficult circumstances. Her father died a few days after her birth and her mother struggled to raise Jane and her seven siblings alone.[44] She grew up in the Seventh Day Adventist (SDA) Church, a mainline church in Kendu Bay, on the shores of Lake Victoria. She went to school up to Form 4[45] and did vocational training, learning the skills of tailoring and catering. Then, she became a 'literature evangelist', selling Christian books, the only (leadership)

---

[44] The story of Jane Akoth as a student at St. Paul's University is recorded in the book: Esther Mombo and Heleen Joziasse, *If You Have No Voice, Just Sing! Narratives of Women's Lives and Theological Education at St. Paul's University* (Limuru, Kenya: Zapf Chancery, 2011), 57–63.

[45] She completed secondary education.

role for women in the SDA. 'I liked going to church and participating in church issues since my childhood. The verse which was important for me during my youth was: "What is that you gain if you get the whole world and you miss that promised everlasting life"'.[46] Her family was not able to support Jane in further studies and hence, she chose to get married. The couple moved to Nairobi because of job opportunities for the husband and Jane gave birth to her first born daughter. This daughter had a medical condition and doctors were not able to diagnose and treat the illness. A neighbor, who was a member of the AINC, introduced her to a woman who was known for her power of prayer and healing. They visited her several times and Jane's daughter became well. Jane decided to join the AINC. Later, when the illness struck the daughter again, she went back to consult the doctors in Nairobi hospitals. Since they couldn't treat the illness, Jane went to consult family members and healers in her home area. She was then introduced to a prophetess of the Mowar Roho Israel Church near her hometown in Kendu Bay. Jane took the daughter to this prophetess and left her to stay on her compound together with other young women who were prayed for. After several months the daughter got well and returned to Nairobi to continue with her education.

Meanwhile Jane enrolled for a Bachelor of Divinity at the Faculty of Theology at St. Paul's University in Limuru, Kenya. In this faculty members of different Protestant traditions including members of the AICs are studying. The study of theology in an ecumenical setting exposed, affirmed and challenged her about her own church tradition and the position of women. As a student Jane was the leader of the Circle of Concerned African Women Theologians, St. Paul's Chapter. While studying she was ordained as the first woman Bishop in the AINC in Nakuru CPO in 2012. She was in charge of all the assemblies in a vast geographical area and at the same time she headed the Education and Training Department in the headquarters. Her ordination into the Bishopric was preceded by a marriage ceremony in the same service. Jane Akoth was transferred in 2013 to Ruiru[47] and from August 2016 she was again transferred to Nairobi, Kayole CPO.

---

[46] From conversation with Jane Akoth 1-2-2017, paraphrasing Matthew 16:26.

[47] The geographical areas of Ruiru, Kiambu and Thika. These are satellite towns of Nairobi.

Bishop Jane Akoth's Leadership in Worship

As noted above worship is central in the AINC and hence, in describing the position of Jane Akoth in leadership, we concentrate on her role in worship. Worship is both an act of reaching to God and sharing issues of life with each other in the community. A leader of worship in the AINC has the authority to preach, to help people to reach God in their needs and to give directions on issues of the people in the community. As a Moderator Bishop Jane is ordained to lead the procession in worship, to lead the congregation in song and dance, to preach, to teach, to lead in public confession and exorcism, to conduct prayers and blessings, and to correct and affirm members, while also giving directions in the interpretation of dreams. Jane performs these tasks in the worship herself or she delegates them to the pastors and priests. Alongside her role in worship Jane Akoth is charged with the administrative tasks in the geographical area. In administration she ensures that each department carries on its tasks as mandated by the church. This includes the finances and the overall running of the assemblies in the administrative area.

The role of the AINC-Moderator Bishop in worship is multi-dimensional. The spiritual dimension is at the center of the endeavor, alongside the social, physical, economic and missional aspect. The procession which is part of the worship reflects a sincere holistic approach to life. It is a public 'walk of witness' to the risen Christ and to the presence of the Holy Spirit. As soldiers in the army of Christ, the AINC-members identify evil spirits and rebuke them through prayer, song and dance, providing healing from both physical and spiritual afflictions. Physically the worship experience acts as a work-out exercise, releasing stress and tension, as well as offering people new energy.

The procession has a missional dimension as well. Through songs and dance people are attracted and invited to join the church and to experience the saving power of Jesus Christ.

Socially the church is a community where difficult issues are shared, for example, disease, death, joblessness and childlessness. In sharing, people support each other through difficult times and search for healing and wholeness in the community. The worship offers also a space to share the joys of life, celebrating together the birth of a child, the healing of a member, employment, schooling, passing of exams and so on.

Economically, the church encourages the members to be industrious, to be involved in businesses, to be more financially independent (esp. the women), and to support each other in times of need through collections and *harambees*.[48]

All these different aspects of worship are embodied in the leadership of Jane Akoth. While living in the slums implies contestation in all aspects of life, through worship with its various dimensions, people make meaning of living in the margins of the city. The places in the city where AINC women and men pray testify to an ambivalent attitude toward wealth and emphasize both the equality of all people in community and the importance and power of a spiritual life in this life and in the hereafter. Jane Akoth manages to bring the voice of women to the center of worship in the midst of ambivalence and contestation.

The Dynamics of Bishop Jane Akoth's Leadership

Jane Akoth's leadership is seen as a model by other women in the AINC and by women in other African Instituted Churches.[49] She is aware of her unique position and she actively seeks out other women to mentor them in leadership. She has earned respect and gained authority even from the top leadership of the AINC. Her success can be ascribed to the way in which she is negotiating her position daily. In a context where patriarchal structures are thriving, due to missionary, Christian and cultural legacies, she practices agency to resist oppression on the basis of gender and ethnicity.

Agency is demonstrated in different ways: She is the only woman in the AINC who is theologically trained, among a few trained men leaders. Her theological training and her biblical training have helped her to position herself within the AINC, without estranging herself from the faith practices and the worship in the AINC. Backed by the church regulations, she manages to resist the ideologies and theologies that deny her a leadership position as a woman. She emphasizes that God created men and women in God's own image and likeness and that members of the AINC are brothers and sisters who seek God through repentance and are called to serve in different categories. Moreover, with her proven skills in business, she has managed to fit in the expected leadership style of the church and at the same time she meets the requirements of being a role model for

---

[48] A *harambee* (Kiswahili) is an event organized in a community to raise funds.

[49] For instance, in the Nomya Luo Church, the Mowar Roho Israel Church, and the African Divine Church, women are not allowed to lead the congregation.

women while being industrious.[50] When need is there, Jane Akoth crosses church boundaries and invokes the healing powers of a prophetess in another church to search for recovery of her daughter. Asked how she feels about her leadership Jane is positive about her position, but she also doesn't shy away from raising the dynamics and complexities of this leadership. Part of the complexities arise from what appears to be the earlier described disconnect between what is written in the regulations of the AINC, published in 1993 within a particular cultural context, about the roles and responsibilities of women on the one hand, and the equality of men and women in leadership, reflected in the Kenyan society on the other hand. The overall spirit of the church regulations is that of women being leaders in the supportive role, women who are industrious and should be able to support the church and the family materially and spiritually. The biblical passages that are cited in the church constitution of the AINC mainly support this female role. This is amplified by the prescription in the church regulations that succession is hereditary, especially for the office of Archbishop/High Priest which is passed on from father to son, while all appointments and ordinations in the AINC are done by the High Priest himself.

AUTHORITY AND NEGOTIATION

Within this context Jane shows how she is able to fit in both the public and the private spheres and she does this using her negotiation skills. On the one hand she takes the spirit of the church regulations by the letter, and on the other hand she is able to take on authority to officiate the spiritual and organizational role as Moderator Bishop. For example, on 22 October 2016, Jane Akoth organized and led the procession in Kayole. She preached and introduced a new male Bishop who was appointed and ordained by the Archbishop/High Priest.

Culturally, it seems that the implementation of the notion of co-leadership has helped many women to reach the ranks of leadership. Jane Akoth was ordained as Moderator Bishop together with her husband, and although he is not involved in the activities of the church, as co-Bishop he is at the same level with his spouse. This seems to prevent tension in marriage. Yet, women leaders often have to negotiate between private and public responsibilities, to be able to spend time outside the family to do

---

[50] Since in the AINC leaders work on voluntary basis, Jane Akoth is a full-time employee of a company.

the work of the church and to pray in the church. Moreover, the culturally and biblically instigated requirements for attending worship, let alone for ritual leadership, include bodily purity. As a relatively young woman and a Bishop Moderator, Jane Akoth has the authority to organize the church calendar to suit her body cycle. She has the power to delegate duties without making known she is in her period.

It is from these observations in relation to worship that we conclude that Moderator Bishop Jane embodies contestation. While the constitution and her theological education support her being Bishop, she struggles with the way the Bible and her culture are used for interpreting ritual leadership. Her position in leadership raises controversy and debate about her position as a woman and a church leader. Hence, she lives a life of negotiation within herself and in the community she is leading. In her role as Moderator Bishop she destabilizes the categories of theory and practice, of organized/chaotic, rational/spiritual, Christian/cultural, transcendent/immanent, rich/poor, civilized/primitive, pure/impure, urban/rural, private and public. In doing this she proves to shape postcolonial feminist leadership. She problematizes, hybridizes and undermines polar distinctions and hegemonic thinking.[51]

CONCLUSION

In this chapter we observe how Moderator Bishop Jane Akoth, who as a woman grew up in the margins of society, now works in church leadership in a church which is located in the margins of Nairobi. Her leadership constitutes both a challenge and an affirmation to her members which she serves. Out of the margins she managed to study to a level which is higher than most of the members. This education offered her the opportunity to move from the margins of her church, to the center. She is able to earn a living, not from the church, but from other engagements including business with which she supports her family and the church. In her leadership role she speaks to the members using her acquired knowledge. She challenges the members of the congregation not to be complacent with the *mabati* churches in the informal settlements, but to seek ways for transforming their situations, including the improvement of the construction of the *mabati* churches. This transformation is at the same time a process

---

[51] Robert S. Heaney, *From Historical to Critical Post-Colonial Theology: The Contribution of John S. Mbiti and Jesse N. K. Mugambi* (Eugene: Wipf and Stock Publishers, 2015), 29.

of healing and spiritual wholeness for the members. Through her agency Jane Akoth has been able to grow and develop herself to this level of leadership in the AINC. In this chapter we concentrated on Bishop Akoth's power in leading worship and noted the different ways that she negotiates the use of the culture and the Bible in her church. The story of Bishop Jane Akoth and all other AINC-women in leadership positions is proof of a hybridized theology which destabilizes Western forms of hegemony and African patriarchal hegemony. A study and interpretation of the leadership of an individual woman such as Bishop Akoth shows the agency of women in leadership. It is only through openness to subjective and experiential knowledge that marginalized voices, such as the voice of Jane Akoth, are heard.

CHAPTER 7

Discipleship as Living Out Baptism: A Dalit Public Engagement with Theology of Bonhoeffer

Raj Bharat Patta

DALIT CHRISTIANS: BY FAITH CHRISTIAN, BY LAW NON-CHRISTIAN, BY EXPERIENCE OUTCASTE: DISCERNING THEOLOGICALLY

Every Dalit Christian, after conversion, is a sum total of several identities. This is the case especially because of the discrimination and exclusion done to Christians of Scheduled Caste origin by the Indian state over the last 66 years. By not ascribing the Scheduled Caste (SC) status on Dalit Christians, it has brought to the front several challenges to the identity of Dalit Christians. The 1950 Presidential Order of the Indian Constitution deprives justice and equal rights to Dalits who were converted to Christianity and Islam and denied them the Scheduled Caste status unlike other Dalit brothers and sisters who were converted to Hinduism, Buddhism and Sikhism.

R. B. Patta (✉)
Lincoln Theological Institute, University of Manchester,
Manchester, UK

In this context, Christians of Scheduled Caste origins, despite their loyalty to their Christian faith, have registered themselves as Hindus in their caste certificates, in order to avail the benefits given by the government, such as educational scholarships, opportunities to contest in legislative elections in reserved constituencies and security from Prevention of Atrocities Act (POA) of SC/ST in times of atrocities. This multiple identity is something unique to Dalit Christians alone, for their counterparts like Dalit Hindus, Dalit Sikhs and Dalit Buddhists all enjoy both the constitutional rights of Scheduled Castes and the freedom of religion by openly professing and practising their own faith, in this land of secularism.

Ashok Kumar and Rowena Robinson therefore explain the dual identity (Hindu and Christian) among Dalit Christians 'as a symbol of the group's sub-ordination/marginality and also a product of structurally imposed marginality. As a product, dual identity emerges as the outcome of the need to cope with concerns about identity and social marginality.'[1] This calls for a discussion on this multiple identity within Dalit Christians which is considered as both a challenge and a prospect; it is a challenge in terms of the imposed marginality and struggle that these Dalit Christians undergo and prospect in terms of expressing their resilience to the continuing exclusion and discrimination that they undergo. However, the ambiguities in the identity of Dalit Christians have some serious theological implications in the life of the Indian church.

These multiple identities firstly bring to the fore the question of baptism. Dalit Christians who are by faith Christian and by law are Hindu struggle with the concept of baptism. They partake in all aspects of the life of the church, by attending the church and other related activities. But the church enforces that unless they are baptized, they are not full members of the church, by which case they are denied participating in the governance of the churches, which has to deal with legal-related issues, because they are not 'full Christian.'

Secondly, the credibility of Dalit Christians in terms of their discipleship is put to question. They are criticized for compromising the 'Christian' values for the sake of availing some affirmative actions and registering themselves legally as Hindus. Since they are not baptized members of the

[1] Ashok M. Kumar and Rowena Robinson, 2010, "Legally Hindu: Dalits Lutheran Christians of Coastal Andhra Pradesh." In Robinson, Rowena & Kujur, Joseph Marianus (eds), *Margins of Faith, Dalits & Tribal Christianity in India*. New Delhi: Sage Publications, p. 150.

church, the weddings of these people are not performed in the church by the local pastor and on the other hand they are performed in community halls with Christian liturgy and the wedding is registered by a secular marriage registrar. The discipleship of these Christians is termed as 'diluted discipleship.'

Thirdly, the citizenship of Dalit Christians in India is further tested. A Dalit Christian continues to undergo alienation, humiliation and marginalization and suffers from five-fold discrimination: (1) by the hostile Hindu society, for they are from an untouchable community, (2) by the unfriendly government since they affirm their faith in Christianity as Dalit, (3) by the fellow Hindu Dalits for availing the benefits of Scheduled Caste though they don't practice Hindu faith, (4) by the unredeemed caste-minded Christian community, who think Dalit Christians are lower to them on the caste pyramid and (5) by the sub-groups of the Dalit Christians themselves who think they are chosen ones and who sacrificed their benefits for faith, for they think these people were unfaithful to the commitment of Christian faith for subscribing to be legally Hindu. Gopal Guru calls such a status as 'citizens in permanent exile,' for their dream of equal citizenship is always unfulfilled and have been excluded in civil society and in political domain.

These issues therefore help us to discuss what is baptism, discipleship and citizenship theologically, and how should we understand them in the context of Dalit Christian reality. In this search, an engagement with Bonhoeffer becomes handy, for he theologically discussed these issues in the context of growing state oppression and oppressive regimes. Bonhoeffer was a creative theologian in his own times who spoke about baptism and discipleship and linked it to the very understanding of citizenship, which has public theological relevance for our times today in the context of 'Christianity and citizenship in India.'

My social and theological location comes from Dalit Lutheran Christian context in Andhra Pradesh in India, and therefore I reflect from those perspectives publicly here in this chapter.

READING PUBLICLY MODERN ACTS OF APOSTLES

Though Luther has used words like 'disciple' and 'discipleship' in his translation of Scriptures, the theme 'discipleship' was not popular in the Lutheran theological language until Bonhoeffer made it more vocal and public with his *The Cost of Discipleship*. Therefore, as a Lutheran offering to this conversation, there can be no better way than to bring in the contributions of a young Lutheran Pastor Dietrich Bonhoeffer (1906–1945), who passionately and prophetically wrote about discipleship in the fragile and hostile world, in which he lived and was killed. Most of Bonhoeffer's letters and writings were published posthumously after his martyrdom, and his literature is a pool of rich resource of theology, ethics, church and spirituality, which has its continuing relevance on the life of Christian discipleship. Reinhold Niebuhr, in his tribute to Bonhoeffer, wrote that 'the story of Bonhoeffer is worth recording, for it belongs to the modern acts of apostles.'[2] Truly the life, witness and contributions of Bonhoeffer belong to the modern acts of apostles, for he lived out what he believed, and lived as a disciple of Jesus Christ, exemplifying what it means to live out one's baptism.

Bonhoeffer is not known for penning bulky textbooks on systematic theology, nor is known for articulating philosophical treatises, but is well known globally for actualizing faith in Jesus Christ into reality, for translating faith into praxis, for living on what he preached and preached what he lived. He kept living even in his death and kept inspiring communities to ground their faith in Jesus Christ and address the challenges of one's own times. Though Bonhoeffer never used the word 'public theology,' all his theological literature belongs to the genre of public theology, for he spoke about faith in Jesus Christ for a 'world coming of age', aiming for a 'religionless Christianity.' He always attempted a secular interpretation of the gospel of Jesus,Christ, for he recognized that Christ's message is a public message for the entire world. The repressive state, church and academy served as his publics, to which Bonhoeffer tried to address, challenge and critique from his Christian discipleship positioning. He was bold in challenging the authoritative state and its regime for its racist and discriminatory practices and rule; he was bold in calling for confessions from the church for her callousness and for bowing down to modern Caesar of their times; he was bold in calling Christians to effectively disciple Jesus Christ grounding their faith not on 'cheap grace' but on 'costly grace'; and he was bold in challenging the narratives of modernity by drawing the public relevance of Christ in a secular world. His 'speaking truth to the powers,'

[2] Rienhold Niebuhr, "The Death of a Martyr," *Christianity and Crisis,* June 25, 1945, p. 6, as cited in Geffrey B. Kelly & F. Burton Nelson. 2003. *The Cost of Moral Leadership: The Spirituality of Bonhoeffer,* Michigan: William B. Eerdmans Publishing Company, p. 1.

not just to the church but to the powers of State, makes him a genuine public theologian par excellence, having paid with his life for his public courage. All of these (ad)ventures of Bonhoeffer make him a public theologian who worked relentlessly to 'spiritualize politics' and 'politicize spirituality.'

There are several facets of Bonhoeffer's theology, and it would be a herculean task to consolidate all of his writings into one capsule and present it here; however, since the parameters of this chapter arise around 'Baptism' and 'discipleship,' I would like to present to you two important theological reflections of Bonhoeffer on these themes. The first is a letter written for the occasion of his grandnephew Dietrich's baptism from prison and the second one is from his classic 'Cost of Discipleship,' in which he makes a distinction between cheap and costly grace. Both these theological literary sources help us to un-pick several threads knitted into it and seek relevance for our understanding on 'discipleship' and 'living our baptism.' May I remind you, Bonhoeffer is not a dogmatic theologian delving on the details of the doctrine but was more a practical theologian who publicized the doctrine, in this case the sacrament of baptism, into the everyday walk of life. Followed by this, I discuss Bonhoeffer's understanding of discipleship in the light of Luther's understanding of discipleship and bring out some convergences from their engagements. Finally, I draw out three points of public relevance, which are helpful in our trilateral conversations here.

This public reading of Bonhoeffer's theology is, from an Asian, Indian, Dalit, subaltern, Lutheran, public theological positioning, where my subjectivities are felt throughout the expositions here. I also need to mention that it was Bonhoeffer's dream to sojourn to India to get exposed to the non-violent resistance movements against the colonial powers, but unfortunately, he could not make it to India. Therefore, 'here I stand' out of that 'unfulfilled dream' making an exposition on the Bonhoeffer's theology of discipleship. The 'public' is used firstly in Habermasian perspective, which is 'a space where critical opinion is made.' Secondly, I use 'public' in a public theological perspective, where 'faith's relevance is felt in public' and where 'public is interrogated by faith.' Thirdly, I use it in an ecumenical perspective, where 'public' is understood as trans-denominational sense against the 'privatization of faith.'

BONHOEFFER'S BAPTISM LETTER TO DIETRICH:
A CALL TO DISCIPLESHIP

Bonhoeffer's 'Letters and Papers from Prison' is a pool of startling theological literature, which reflects the tenacity of the varied textures of theology, that withstood suffering, imprisonment, conspiracy, death and life. Out of these letters, the letter written to Dietrich, his grandnephew, for his baptism during May 1944, which is entitled as 'Thoughts on the Day of Baptism of Dietrich Wilhelm Rudiger Bethge', speaks about the pastoral function and discipleship as living out baptism. In this letter he mentions that he could only participate from a distance at Dietrich's parents wedding, at his birth and at his baptism; however, he expressed hope that he looks forward to Dietrich's future with 'great confidence and cheerful hope.' There are several biblical verses that Bonhoeffer reminds Dietrich of in his letter exhorting him from the Word of God. He speaks about their ancestral past, their Christian heritage and legacy, their grounding in virtues of the gospel, about growing urbanization, about church and about faith, all of which makes this letter as one of the powerful public theological statements of Bonhoeffer.

At this point, it would be of great worth to read verbatim the final section of this letter, for it conveys the essence of discipleship and living out baptism.

> Today you will be baptized a Christian. All those great ancient words of the Christian proclamation will be spoken over you, and the command of Jesus Christ to baptize will be carried out on you, without your knowing anything about it. But we are once again being driven right back to the beginnings of our understanding. Reconciliation and redemption, regeneration and the Holy Spirit, love of our enemies, cross and resurrection, life in Christ and Christian discipleship—all these things are so difficult and so remote that we hardly venture any more to speak of them.

Bonhoeffer then laments over the eccentric and self-centric nature of the church, which seeks to keep up the status quo of its institutionalized structures. He goes on to say,

> In the traditional words and acts we suspect that there may be something quite new and revolutionary, though we cannot as yet grasp or express it. That is our own fault. Our Church, which has been fighting in these years only for its self-preservation, as though that were an end in itself, is incapable

of taking the word of reconciliation and redemption to mankind and the world. Our earlier words are therefore bound to lose their force and cease, and our being Christians today will be limited to two things: prayer and righteous action among men. All Christian thinking, speaking and organizing must be born anew out of this prayer and action. By the time you have grown up, the church's form will have changed greatly. We are not yet out of the melting-pot, and any attempt to help the church prematurely to a new expansion of its organization will merely delay its conversion and purification. It is not for us to prophesy the day (though the day will come) when men will once more be called so to utter the word of God that the world will be changed and renewed by it.

Bonhoeffer then speaks about the need for a public language, understandable by all people in the public sphere, which would address the needs of our times. He continues to say:

It will be a new language, perhaps quite non-religious, but liberating and redeeming—as was Jesus' language; it will shock people and yet overcome them by its power; it will be the language of a new righteousness and truth, proclaiming God's peace with men and the coming of his kingdom. 'They shall fear and tremble because of all the good and all the prosperity I provide for it' (Jer 33.9). Till then the Christian cause will be a silent and hidden affair, but there will be those who pray and do right and wait for God's own time. May you be one of them, and may it be said of you one day, 'The path of the righteousness is like the light of dawn, which shines brighter and brighter till full day.' (Prov 4.18)[3]

Let me remind you, Dietrich would have been just few days old as he was baptized in Lutheran tradition as an infant, and yet Bonhoeffer writes deep theological stuff on this occasion to this infant Dietrich. Can the baby Dietrich read and comprehend his letter? The clue to understand this question is answered when Bonhoeffer writes that Jesus' baptismal command will be pronounced 'without our knowing about it.' On the one hand, the reason Bonhoeffer wrote this letter to the infant Dietrich is his belief in, and affirmation of, the role of faith that comes from God, which is a happening of God in every human, for faith is God's prerogative in every human life, which is reaffirmed at baptism. On the other hand, this letter calls to mind the pastoral role of the parents and the church in

---

[3] Dietrich Bonhoeffer. 1973. *Letters and Papers from Prison,* London: SCM Press, pp. 299–300.

nurturing the baptismal values in an infant, for it is the parents who are called to understand the essence of his letter and to make him realize the grace of God in his life. Finally, when Dietrich grows old, this baptism letter to him would serve as a barometer of faith to check his discipleship quotient in his life.

On analysing this baptism letter, one can recognize that there are several themes woven into this letter, and each of those threads needs careful consideration and explanation. However, in light of deciphering discipleship as living out baptism, I would like to draw upon three characteristics of discipleship, which are pertinent for our trilateral conversations as churches.

Discipleship as Reaffirming the Kerygmatic Potency of the Community

In his baptism letter, Bonhoeffer reminds the infant Dietrich and the community around him about the incompetence of the church and Christians in communicating the revolutionary meaning embedded in essence of redemption and reconciliation. In a way, Bonhoeffer is trying to relocate the baptismal setting as a space of confession for the church and community around the baptismal baby, in light of the church not being able to provide an authentic Christ community. Baptism is an act of incorporating a person into the body of Christ, and therefore discipleship is overcoming our in ability as a church to communicate the revolutionary gospel in Jesus Christ. Why are we not able to grasp or express those meanings in the gospel? Bonhoeffer would say, because the 'Church has been fighting all these years for its self-preservation, as though that is the end in itself.' Frits De Lange would call that 'Kerygmatic impotence.'[4] Self-preservation is not the duty and an end in itself for the church, for she is called to live for others and reach out to others. Discipleship therefore is recognition of the incapability as a community, acknowledging our faults and confessing and overcoming them. Our discipleship in Christ is shaped by our nurturing community, and is mutually dependent on the participating members, and so a corporal confession of our faults as a community is envisaged in discipleship.

---

[4] Frits De Lange, "Waiting for the Word: The Churches Embarrassment in Speaking about God," in John W. de Gruchy. 1997. *Bonhoeffer for a New Day*, Michigan: William B. Eerdmans, p. 99.

There is a kerygmatic potency among the baptismal community, which has to be affirmed so that authentic and experiential meanings of redemption, reconciliation, cross, resurrection, life, Holy Spirit, Christ, love and discipleship will be recovered and expressed.

Discipleship as Reliving Faith with a Coherence of Prayer and Action

The second characteristic of discipleship seen in this baptism letter from Bonhoeffer is that of reliving our faith in Christ by striking a coherence of prayer and action. The mark of Christian discipleship is based on prayer and righteous actions among people, which goes hand in hand in reliving one's faith. He says, 'All Christian thinking, speaking and organizing must be born anew out of this prayer and action.' Christian thought, speech and communitarian activity of organizing are to be born again and born anew out of these marks. Bonhoeffer as a disciple of Christ practised such a faith where prayer and action went hand in hand, for prayer is an inward expression to God, and action is an outward expression shown among people. He qualifies action by saying that it needs be 'righteous action,' which addresses systemic injustices, powers and principalities and all such forces existing in our times. Prayer and righteous action are the two sides of discipleship and will always exist one with another. It was observed that, 'Although there is no one answer to what is intended by the "action for justice" to which he referred in his baptismal sermon, three dimensions seem consistently to emerge from his writings. Bonhoeffer advocates an unabashed solidarity with the oppressed, concrete steps to liberate the victims of unjust societies, and the willingness to suffer for the sake of Christ, all related to what for him was the "costly grace" of following Jesus Christ.'[5] This reveals Bonhoeffer's spirituality, where his faith is guided and actualized with a coherence of prayer and action. Our prayers should be seen in our actions, and our actions should be founded on our prayers: this is the essence of Christian discipleship.

[5] Geffrey B. Kelly, "Prayer and Action for Justice: Bonhoeffer's Spirituality" in John W. de Gruchy (ed.) 1999. *The Cambridge Companion to Dietrich Bonhoeffer,* Cambridge: Cambridge University Press, p. 261.

Discipleship as Rearticulating the Gospel of Christ in a New Language

The third characteristic of discipleship is to rearticulate the gospel of Christ in a new language, with a kerygmatic potency understandable to all people. Bonhoeffer qualifies that new language as primarily 'non-religious,' for thus far the language has been very churchy and dogmatic. 'The world come of age' demands a new language which is going to be 'non-religious,' for in challenging the project of modernity, a new language is necessitated. The new language is going to be 'liberating and redeeming,' which has been the yearning of our contexts. Bonhoeffer qualifies that new language with that of 'Jesus' language,' for Jesus' language was the language of the people, the excluded and those on the margins, for 'it will shock people and yet overcome them by its people's power.' The new language is going to be a 'language of new righteousness and truth, proclaiming God's peace with people and the coming of his kingdom.' Discipleship therefore is to capture and learn this new language to articulate the gospel of Christ relevantly, contemporarily, concretely and contextually. The active involvement in a resistance movement provided the needed impetus for Bonhoeffer to articulate the gospel in a new language, for 'Jesus—a man for others.' It was observed, 'his statements about the coming of a "non-religious" Christianity are a caution to the church to convert to Jesus Christ and patiently wait with perseverance in prayer and courage in deeds until it can "once more be called to utter the Word of God that the world will be changed and renewed by it."'[6] So discipleship demands a self-introspection, a conversion experience to utter and rearticulate the gospel of Christ in a new language, not with mere semantics, but more with pragmatics in the language of the gospel.

Thus, Bonhoeffer's baptism letter written from his prison communicates an immense theology of discipleship and its relationship with baptism. Bonhoeffer could have communicated much more on baptism, but in writing a baptism letter, he communicates that authentic discipleship is in living one's baptism to its fullest sense, with Christ and the word of God at the centre and with a passion to translate the gospel into a new language, appropriate to the context. His theology of discipleship is not a static theology, but a dynamic theology which keeps evolving and strengthening in the journey of faith.

---

[6] Geffrey B. Kelly & F. Burton Nelson. 2003. *The Cost of Moral Leadership: The Spirituality of Bonhoeffer,* Michigan: William B. Eerdmans Publishing Company, p. 42.

Peter Selby, commenting on Bonhoeffer's prison letters, says, 'Bonhoeffer's prison letters are those of a person asking whether he or his church, could be able, is able, to live that identity, to declare *Christ for us* with integrity, and to value the baptismal identity above all the other profoundly valuable ones we possess, and resist all that makes those a privilege to be defended at other's expense. The enduring quality of *Letters and Papers from Prison* lies, therefore, in the question with which they leave us, of what it is to be part of that inheritance.'[7] All of his letters from prison have profound theology on varied issues and call the readers of those letters to become answers to those letters, by living them out.

BONHOEFFER'S *THE COST OF DISCIPLESHIP*: LIVING OUT BAPTISM

It was a time when the Nazi government came to power and was oppressing people with discriminatory laws; the church, ever called to speak against the unjust systems of oppression, unfortunately compromised its gospel values and sang chorus with Nazi ideology bowing down to its ruler. It was at this time that Bonhoeffer, along with his Confessing Church, stood with courage in his faith in Jesus Christ and openly opposed injustice, oppression and discrimination. When his 'illegal' seminary was closed down by the rulers, Bonhoeffer penned his famous book *Discipleship* in 1937. This book is a 'pastoral outrage' by Bonhoeffer, incorporating Christocentric spirituality, with a 'secular' reading of scriptures, trying to unpack what it means to be a genuine disciple, following Jesus Christ at a time of struggle. It is interesting to note that the original German title for this book *Nachfolge* means 'following after', with Jesus impled as the one being followed after; a title which bears a close resemblance to Thomas Kempis' classic book *Nachfolge Christi* (The Imitation of Christ, which was one of Bonhoeffer's favourite possessions). Only the English translation carried the word 'cost' in relation to discipleship, for Bonhoeffer eloquently spoke on costly grace and cheap grace. There are several themes that run through this book; however, in light of our conversations on baptism, I want to bring out five main tenets of discipleship as living out baptism as proposed by Bonhoeffer.

---

[7] Peter Selby, "Christianity in a World Come of Age," in John W. de Gruchy (ed.) 1999. *The Cambridge Companion to Dietrich Bonhoeffer,* Cambridge: Cambridge University Press, p. 243.

Discipleship and Costly Grace

'Grace alone' was one of the Reformation principles of Luther, and Bonhoeffer elaborates on this theme by distinguishing between 'cheap grace' and 'costly grace.' With the rise of Hitler to power and with the church following him uncritically, Bonhoeffer recognizes 'cheap grace' within and among Christians. He goes on to say, 'Cheap grace is the deadly enemy of our Church. We are fighting today for costly grace ... Cheap grace is the preaching of forgiveness without requiring repentance, baptism without Church discipline, Communion without confession, absolution without contrition. Cheap grace is grace without discipleship, grace without Cross, grace without Jesus Christ, living and incarnate.'[8] This statement is of profound theology, for it puts discipleship in perspective, for unless it is prophetic, discipleship loses its essence and will only ply with cheap grace.

In contrast to this cheap grace, Bonhoeffer presents what he meant by costly grace, for discipleship is a matter of costly grace and he says, 'Costly grace is the gospel which must be *sought* again and again, the gift which must be *asked* for, the door at which a man must *knock*. Such a grace is *costly* because it calls us to follow, and it is grace because it calls us to follow *Jesus Christ*. It is costly because it costs a man his life, it is grace because it gives a man the only true life. It is costly because it condemns sin, and grace because it justifies the sinner. Above all, it is *costly* because it cost God the life of His Son: "ye were bought at a price," and what has cost God much cannot be cheap for us. Above all, it is *grace* because God did not reckon His Son too dear a price to pay for our life but delivered Him up for us. Costly grace is the Incarnation of God.'[9] Discipleship, therefore, has to imbibe, inculcate and practice this costly grace, for discipleship is 'Jesus Christ alone.' Baptism as a sacrament of grace allows the recipient, in faith to grow in the discipleship of a costly grace overcoming the easy-going ramifications and manifestations of cheap grace. 'Grace alone' is truly synonymous to 'Jesus alone' and discipleship is solely following Jesus alone.

Discipleship and the Call

In his next chapter, 'The call to discipleship,' Bonhoeffer defines the content of discipleship, as 'following and running along behind Jesus Christ,' and seeks a response to faith or discipleship as 'only total obedience to the

---

[8] Dietrich Bonhoeffer. 1948. *The Cost of Discipleship,* London: SCM Press, pp. 37–38.
[9] Ibid., p. 39.

call of Jesus Christ.' He links discipleship as single obedience to the word of Jesus Christ, where Christ makes the offer to humankind and not the other way, bringing 'self-preservation' of the churches and 'self-centredness' of Christians to scrutiny. He goes on to say, 'Discipleship means adherence to Christ, and, because Christ is the object of that adherence, it must take the form of discipleship. An abstract Christology, a doctrinal system, a general religious knowledge on the subject of grace or on the forgiveness of sins, renders discipleship superfluous, and in fact they positively exclude any idea of discipleship whatever, and are essentially inimical to the whole conception of following Christ ... Christianity without the living Christ is inevitably Christianity without discipleship, and Christianity without discipleship is always Christianity without Christ... Discipleship without Jesus Christ is a way of our own choosing. It may be an ideal way, it may even lead to martyrdom, but it is devoid of all promise. Jesus will certainly reject it.'[10] It is all about 'Jesus alone' in discipleship, for Bonhoeffer by articulating this he was contesting the project of modernity which has rejected the spiritual essence in Christ in the name of enlightenment, rationality and scientific temperaments. Call, obedience discipleship, Christ and Christianity are all part and parcel of the Christian ethos.

In a similar note Bonhoeffer also proposes that 'Only those who obey can believe, and only those who believe can obey,' by which he knits a link between faith and obedience, which again are the ingredients of discipleship. In the context of baptismal conversations, one can recognize the relationship of faith, obedience and sacrament, for they all go hand in hand, and all of those come into validity, when discipleship is solely led and governed by Jesus alone.

Discipleship and the Cross

If discipleship was solely 'Jesus alone,' Bonhoeffer then would say such an allegiance leads to Cross. He quotes the saying of Jesus, 'if anyone follows me, let him deny himself, take up his cross and follow me,' and extends the understanding of following or discipleship to the cross event. In denying oneself, one ceases to see himself and would see more of Christ, and following Christ would be in total obedience to the word of Christ. Bonhoeffer brings in the understanding of suffering and forgiveness

[10] Ibid., pp. 51–52.

related to Cross, for he says, 'the call to follow Christ always means a call to share the work of forgiving men their sins. Forgiveness is the Christ-like suffering which is the Christian's duty to bear.'[11] This necessitates discipleship as participating in the Christ-like suffering in the community and in sharing in the forgiveness of peoples' sins, which is done by Christ's act on the Cross.

In elaborating further on cross and suffering, he says, 'Suffering then is the badge of the true Christian. The disciple is not above his master. Following Christ means *passio passive*, suffering because we have to suffer … if we refuse to take up our cross and submit to suffering and rejection at the hands of men, we forfeit our fellowship with Christ and have ceased to follow Him. But if we lose our lives in His service and carry our cross, we shall find our lives again. The opposite of discipleship is to be ashamed of Christ and His cross and all the offence which the cross brings in its train. Discipleship means allegiance to the suffering Christ, and it is therefore not at all surprising that Christians should be called upon to suffer.'[12] Therefore, discipleship is not to be ashamed of the cross event, but to seek an allegiance with Christ's suffering and participate in the suffering of the world created by injustice and discrimination. Locating the Christian church among suffering is the call of discipleship, for the church happens among the suffering and amidst cross events.

Discipleship and the Individual

Bonhoeffer then emphasizes that the call from Jesus Christ makes people become an individual, for such a calling into discipleship is a call for an intimate relationship with Christ. Christ as the Mediator between God and humanity is also a mediator between humanity and reality; therefore, any contact established with neighbours is through Christ and by following him. Bonhoeffer says, 'If we take Him and His word and dare to become individuals, our reward is the fellowship of the Church.'[13] The intention of becoming an individual is not to remain in isolation in the world, nor to become individualistic, but to be part of the community, who are all called by Christ, the church.

[11] Ibid., p. 74.
[12] Ibid., pp. 74–75.
[13] Ibid., p. 84.

Though the disciple is called to publicly show forth one's discipleship, Bonhoeffer also speaks about the 'secret discipline,' the hidden dimension of discipleship. One needs to hide oneself from themselves and simply follow the leader, the Christ. In this journey, he says, 'only those who have died after the old man through Christ and are given a new life by following Him and having fellowship with Him ... the love of Christ crucified, who delivers our old man to death, is the love which lives in those who follow Him.'[14] Therefore discipleship is leaving out the old self to death and springing up with Christ, and in Christ, into a new life and new community of Christ. This is the very essence of baptism, for the old self is buried, and a new being is resurrected in this experience. Discipleship is therefore strongly embedded into the very understanding of baptism, the purpose of which is to live it out.

Discipleship and Baptism

'Christ's calling to follow him' as recorded in the synoptic Gospels, according to Bonhoeffer, is equivalent to what St Paul speaks of 'baptism,' and thereby positions discipleship and baptism in a common ground of spirituality. Baptism became synonymous with the literal following of Christ during the times of Jesus Christ, and therefore it becomes an extension to following Christ in our times. He reminds that baptism is not an offering of the human made to Christ, but 'an offer made by Christ to man,' thereby making the sacrament as the gift of grace, for in baptism, the disciple becomes 'Christ's own possession.' For Bonhoeffer says, 'The baptized Christian has ceased to belong to the world and is no longer its slave. He belongs to Christ alone, and his relationship with the world is mediated through Him.'[15] In baptism the disciple is in relationship with the world by the mediation of Christ and has to reflect Christ in their dealings with it, where the 'old self is died along with the old world.' Baptism for Bonhoeffer is 'sharing in the Christ of Cross,' and 'partaking in the death of Christ.' Baptism in the name of Christ is an invitation into the death of Christ, where forgiveness and justification are assured.

On the other hand, baptism for Bonhoeffer is a visible public act of obedience, where the disciple is 'visibly grafted into the body of Christ.' Bonhoeffer, by this exposition of baptism as a public act of obedience,

[14] Ibid., p. 139.
[15] Ibid., p. 175.

counters the privatization of faith, and brings in the public relevance of the sacrament, for the act of Christ is public and has a reach beyond the confines of the church. He further explains that the disciples who are received by Christ in baptism 'live in the visible community of Christ.' It is the baptized disciples who constitute the 'visible community of Christ,' for such a community's calling is to resist evil the society.

Bonhoeffer emphasizes on the finality of the sacrament, and in the case of infant baptism, he opines that the sacrament of baptism should be administered to infants only when there is a reasonable nurture for the child to renew the faith that was 'accomplished once for all when he is baptized.' Bonhoeffer reminds the importance of the community of Christians, among whom the baptized disciple will grow, for he thinks baptizing a child and not bringing them up in the life of the living community is an 'abuse of the sacrament.' Discipleship thus requires a committed Christian community for the growth of a baptized disciple, whereby discipleship becomes a communitarian act of faith.

Towards the end of his book, Bonhoeffer concludes that the goal of discipleship is to 'become as Christ,' 'recover the dignity of the image of God' and thereby become 'imitators of God.' *The Cost of Discipleship* is a book that communicates Bonhoeffer's spirituality and invites the readers to follow Jesus Christ even to death, and witness for the cause of truth and justice. Discipleship is living out baptism, living truly for Christ.

Relevance of Bonhoeffer's Theology of Discipleship Today

A public reading of Bonhoeffer's theology of discipleship has opened up several key areas and issues for our conversations here, which are pertinent and relevant for our collective witness today. Allow me to present three important manifestations of discipleship which are contextually relevant for our churches today.

Towards a Public Kerygma

Our contexts today demand the seeking of a relationship between discipleship and citizenship, discipleship and spirituality, and discipleship and solidarity, for we need to engage in theological conversations on these themes, for we need a strong public theology for our times. Baptism as a Christ's act, as a public act and as a communitarian act is of great significance in our spirituality. We need to seek convergences in our faith traditions in this regard, and discipleship as living out baptism should become an inspiring factor for our faith communions. Discipleship as affirming in the kerygmatic potency of the visible community in Christ, as reliving faith in coherence with prayer and action and as rearticulating the gospel of Christ in a new language, is very significant for our times.

In the context of Dalit Christians' struggles for 'equal citizenry' what then should be the public kerygma of the church today? There are several challenges that the Christian faith communities are facing; firstly from within there has been a growing eccentric trend with more emphasis on the inward looking, giving preference to issues like healing, miracles, prosperity and life after death. Secondly, from the outside, there are issues like religious fundamentalism, violence in the name of religions, communalism, racism, casteism, gender discrimination, climate injustice and so on. Therefore, in such a context public theological articulations and praxis become more and more important than before, and a public kerygma is the need of the hour. Bonhoeffer's 'religionless Christianity' or a 'secular interpretation of Christ' forms the grammar and content of this 'new language,' so that the gospel speaks to the public around us. Our conversations should inspire us to articulate that public kerygma, which is amphibious in nature, holding together both ecclesial and secular, both prayer and just actions, both visibility and hidden-ness, and both baptism and discipleship. Discipleship today is to speak open the public kerygma for our times.

The role of the church is to affirm the equality of her people and this necessitates the resistance of all forms of exclusion done to Dalit Christians, be it doctrinally or existentially. Dalit Christians should not stay on the margins of inclusion, but should be integrated into the whole public sphere, for they are equal in every right and no caste, no religion and no dogma should prevent them not to be the 'full members' of the public sphere. The church's public kerygma should be to strive for justice and equality for its 'non-members' and should contest all moral judgements made on people in the name of 'diluted discipleship,' for both baptism and discipleship are God's prerogative. When churches become hubs of inclusion, peoples' citizenry is affirmed, for the self-respect, self-dignity and self-identity of Dalit Christians are recovered and recognized.

Towards a Public Baptism

In proposing a public baptism, the intention is not to promote 'mass conversions' or 'mass baptisms,' but rather to seek the relevance of baptism in our public spheres. As Bonhoeffer proposed, following Christ is a visible act, and so should be our baptism, by which the call is to seek a public relevance of our sacraments, here baptism. Baptism is not a mere 'churchy act' but a public act, for the disciples are called to live out baptism as discipleship out in the public. Therefore, in the context of growing divisions among churches in the name of baptism, on the mode and its practice, on the dogma and doctrines, the challenge for us is to make baptism a unifying factor for all those believing in transforming the world. Our baptismal vows need to encourage and inspire us to partake in building communities of justice and peace around us. If we truly believe that baptism is the outward expression of our inward grace, we need to affirm life and channel life to all those people in lifeless situations. Baptism needs to inspire us not to focus merely on sets of doctrines associated with it but to make it a tool for social transformation and liberation, for we are called to overcome attitudes of superiority and exclusive claims and be humble in translating baptism as a means of grace, as a public act of discipleship. By our public act of baptism, we are grafted into the visible community of Christ, whose primary mandate is to live for others, the wider public. Discipleship today is to live out baptism in the public.

In context of Dalit Christians, if by faith they are Christian, the churches should not deny baptism to such people, for baptism is a tool of social empowerment and liberation. For Dalit Christians, the non-Christian identity is not their performed religious identity; their experience as outcastes as a continuing identity is a challenge for the church and society to overcome the marginality and strengthen the resilience of Dalit Christians.

Towards a Public Ecclesia

Bonhoeffer was critical of his own church for bowing down to the empire of Caesar, which was manifested in the oppressive regime of Hitler. He emphatically proclaimed that the church should follow its master Jesus Christ, thus the church should be bold in addressing the discriminatory rules of the State. His call to the churches in his times and to our times is to rise to the occasion of addressing the repressive laws of the church and live out our collective discipleship in the public. In affirming the collective discipleship, the call for the churches today is to affirm Christ in our concreteness, realistically and contextually. This call reminds us to be rooted strongly in Christocentric spirituality, for discipleship is all about Christ. The call for the churches today is to be and become as 'churches for others,' where 'othering' overcomes privilege, and seeks confession and forgiveness. The call for the churches is to locate themselves among the suffering in our localities today, thereby participating in the suffering of Christ and striving for a new life experience. In that pursuit, churches are called to inculcate a perspective, which is 'a view from below,' for those on the margins are partners and collaborators in the mission of God.

The need of the hour in the context of Dalit Christian realities as a public ecclesia is a 'public pastoral outrage' against the forces of injustices, systemic violence and all forms of discrimination that are happening in our situations. Let us contest different forms of empire in our localities and strive for a just society. Our baptism should inspire us to rage with Christ against the powers and principalities that oppress people and creation around us. Bonhoeffer's terms, 'put a spoke in the wheel,' is a call for the churches to resist forces of fundamentalism, casteism, fascism, nepotism and all such forms that exist in our own contexts. This mission should become our pastoral function, nurturing public ecclesia towards just communities so that our baptism becomes a true living for the realization of God's reign here on earth. Discipleship today is coming out openly as public ecclesia, in being and becoming just and inclusive communities.

CONCLUSION

Bonhoeffer's contributions to theology and church are not only decisive features in the history of theology, but also have an ongoing validity for our signs of time too. His life, witness, spirituality, contributions, theology, pastoral practice and even his death all speak voluminously on discipleship in Christ, for his life and martyrdom was his message. Discipleship as living out baptism is a call to keep up a consistency in our faith journey, for baptism calls on the accountability of the community in which the disciple nurtures. The legacy of Bonhoeffer will continue to inspire many generations to come, for he in obedience to the word of Christ, lived, spoke, wrote and died a martyr. If Bonhoeffer were to come alive today, he wouls be publicly contesting the modern empires of capitalism, repressive regimes of our times that oppress people, systemic structures of injustices that exclude and discriminate people, and he would be risking his life for the cause of his discipleship in Christ. May we as citizens inherit his indomitable spirituality, and courageously stand for the values of gospel and live them out as responsible disciples of Jesus Christ today.

In the context of Dalit Christian realities, their faith and their experiences help them to chart out their own understanding of discipleship and citizenship, which are unique and authentic. To be a disciple of Christ, for Dalit Christians their Dalitness and Christian-ness collaborate in their formation, and as 'citizens of permanent exile' they are longing for an inclusive and equal citizenry in the Indian public sphere.

In trying to explore 'What Makes a Good City? Public Theology and Urban Church' (London: Darton Longman Todd, 2009) Elaine Graham and Stephen Lowe start their discussion on the very pertinent distinction of 'citizenship and discipleship.' In defining 'public theology,' they explain it as a theology that holds in creative tension the two poles of 'public' and 'ecclesial,' for 'theology is revealed in divine teaching, [and] it must be tested 'in public.' It is a 'theology of God-in-the-world, *to* the world' (p. 4) where mutual partnerships and conversations with non-ecclesial world are not undermined. Discipleship defines the world of the church and citizenship defines the world of the public.

Prior to Harvey Cox's *Secular City*, it was Augustine of Hippo's *City of God* that projected a public theological framework. The two cities in this *City* issue from humanity's conflicting desires, the love of self and the love of God. These are not two entities of a city; rather, they are two overlapping visions of one city, where the twin vocations of citizenship and discipleship are interwoven. For Augustine, according to Charles Mathews, 'Theology of Public Life' (2008), sin is understood as 'privation,' as in deprivation or isolation of the self from the love of God. In this respect the redemption would be a restoration of 'public-ity,' a turning back to right relationship with God and creation (p. 19). It is the 'common grace' that holds together the citizenship and discipleship of every Christian, in its longing for public theologizing project.

BIBLIOGRAPHY

Barker, H. Gaylon. 2015. *The Cross of Reality: Luther's Theologia Crucis and Bonhoeffer's Christology*. Minneapolis: Fortress.
Bonhoeffer, Dietrich. 1948. *The Cost of Discipleship*. London: SCM Press.
———. 1973. *Letters and Papers from Prison*. London: SCM Press.
Feil, Ernst. 1985. *The Theology of Dietrich Bonhoeffer*. Philadelphia: Fortress Press.

Graham, Elaine, and Stephen L. Lowe. 2009. *What Makes a Good City? Public Theology and Urban Church.* London: Darton Longman Todd.

de Gruchy, John W. 1997. *Bonhoeffer for a New Day.* Michigan: William B. Eerdmans.

———., ed. 1999. *The Cambridge Companion to Dietrich Bonhoeffer.* Cambridge: Cambridge University Press.

Kelly, Geffrey B., and F. Burton Nelson. 2003. *The Cost of Moral Leadership: The Spirituality of Bonhoeffer.* Michigan: William B. Eerdmans.

Kumar, Ashok M., and Rowena Robinson. 2010. Legally Hindu: Dalits Lutheran Christians of Coastal Andhra Pradesh. In *Margins of Faith, Dalits & Tribal Christianity in India,* ed. Rowena Robinson and Joseph Marianus Kujur. New Delhi: Sage Publications.

Luther, Martin. 1519. Lectures on Galatians. In *Luther's Works,* American ed., 1955–1986. Philadelphia: Fortress & St. Louis Concordia.

Mattes, Mark. 2012. Discipleship in Lutheran Perspective. *Lutheran Quarterly* XXVI: 142–163.

Plant, Stephen J. 2014. *Tacking Stock of Bonhoeffer.* Surrey: Ashgate.

Todt, Heinz Eduard. 1993. *Authentic Faith.* Michigan: William B. Eerdmans.

CHAPTER 8

Immanuel Kant Believed in Zombies: Multiculturalism and Spirituality in the Postcolonial City

Chris Shannahan

INTRODUCTION

In his *Critique of Pure Reason* Immanuel Kant revealed his fascination with the 'living dead.' The Enlightenment giant insisted that 'Observations without concepts are blind; concepts without observations are empty.'[1] More than two hundred years later Ulrich Beck expressed a similar interest in zombies, 'we are living in a society … where our basic sociological concepts are becoming … "zombie categories" but social scientists cling onto old concepts long after the life has drained from them.'[2] I have lived,

[1] Immanuel Kant, *Critique of Pure Reason* [1781], trans. Kemp Smith (Norman, NY: St. Martins, 1965), A 51/B 75.

[2] John Slater and George Ritzer, 'Interview with Ulrich Beck' in *Journal of Consumer Culture* (2001) 1:2, 261–277.

C. Shannahan (✉)
Centre for Trust, Peace and Social Relations,
Coventry University, Coventry, UK
e-mail: ac0971@coventry.ac.uk

© The Author(s) 2019
J. Dunn et al. (eds.), *Multiple Faiths in Postcolonial Cities*, Postcolonialism and Religions,
https://doi.org/10.1007/978-3-030-17144-5_8

131

worked and worshipped in the most diverse cities in the UK for the past 30 years. Over this period cultural and religious diversity has become normative but the term 'multiculturalism' has been increasingly appropriated by the political right as a synonym for creeping segregation and a barrier to community cohesion.[3] In spite of the predictions of avowed secularists like Steve Bruce faith has continued to be an important marker of life in many urban communities.[4] Consequently, as a result of the social capital that arises from their deep roots in local communities faith groups have become increasingly visible players in ongoing debates about multiculturalism in the UK.[5]

This chapter will consider the contemporary re-invention of the divisive politics of Empire on the streets of the postcolonial British city and at the despatch box in the House of Commons. The combination of this political discourse with a resurgent Orientalism has given rise to a culture within which difference is increasingly demonised. However I will argue that a critical dialogue with aspects of political theology can pave the way for a life after Empire that is characterised by an affirmation of the liberative potential of difference.

MELANCHOLIA, MIGRANTS AND MYOPIA

The sociologist Paul Gilroy argues that the UK's response to diversity is characterised by a kind of social schizophrenia. On the one hand Britain portrays itself as a welcoming society that rejoices in its cultural and religious diversity but on the other views Black-Britons as a threat to a nostalgic, largely fictional, vision of 'British' culture and an unwanted reminder of the days of Empire.[6]

Gilroy suggests that when the nation is envisaged as a ring-fenced 'camp,' 'Culture as process is arrested … (and) … impoverished by the national obligation to recycle the past … in an essentially unmodified mythic form.'[7] Identity, belonging and community are interwoven with an excluding ethnic essentialism, as we have seen in increasingly toxic debates

---

[3] Steven Vertovec, 'Super-Diversity and Its Implications', *Ethnic and Racial Studies* (2007) 30:6, 1024–1054.

[4] Steve Bruce, *God Is Dead: Secularization in the West* (Oxford: Blackwell, 2002), 3.

[5] Graham Ward and Michael Hoelzl, *The New Visibility of Religion: Studies in Religion and Cultural Hermeneutics* (London: Continuum, 2008).

[6] Paul Gilroy, *After Empire: Melancholia or Convivial Culture?* (Abingdon: Routledge, 2004), 109.

[7] Paul Gilroy, *Against Race* (Cambridge, MA: Harvard University Press, 2000), 84.

about immigration, the Europe-wide refugee crisis of 2015–2016, the dramatic rise in recorded hate-crimes in the aftermath of the UK vote to leave the European Union, the 2016 *Casey Review* into integration commissioned by former British Prime Minister David Cameron and the more recent *2018 Integrated Communities Green Paper*. On the international stage the rhetoric of Donald Trump about Mexicans and Muslims during the US presidential campaign in 2016 played to similar xenophobic insecurity. Just two weeks after his inauguration President Trump signed an executive order temporarily banning citizens from seven majority-Muslim countries (Iraq, Iran, Syria, Somalia, Sudan, Libya and Yemen) from entering the USA. This and the accompanying order denying federal funding to sanctuary cities, which provide support and hospitality to undocumented migrants, exemplify the demonising of difference, which impoverishes life after Empire in the postcolonial city.[8]

The depiction of multiculturalism as the primary cause of alleged residential segregation in British cities and Trump's 'America First' nationalism exemplify the assumptions, which characterised Samuel Huntington's 'clash of civilisations' thesis and its underpinning Orientalism.[9] Particularly pronounced in the artistic and cultural commentary of the colonial area, Orientalist discourse depicted the cultures of the Middle East, the Indian sub-continent and Africa as exotic and alien.[10] The Western depiction of the 'Orient' as alien drew on an essentialised understanding of identity and culture, which pitted Occident and Orient as binary opposites. This unreasonable objectification of the Orient as a singular homogeneous cultural block enabled the forging of a cultural politics within which people of African, Caribbean, South Asian or Middle Eastern heritage were framed as cultural outsiders who disrupted the so-called cultural purity of European societies. Cultural, existential and ontological distinctions were

---

[8] Web sites http://www.npr.org/2017/01/31/512439121/trumps-executive-order-on-immigration-annotated; https://www.theatlantic.com/news/archive/2017/01/trump-immigration-order-muslims/514844/#exec%20order; https://www.washingtonpost.com/news/volokh-conspiracy/wp/2017/01/26/constitutional-problems-with-trumps-executive-order-on-sanctuary-cities/?utm_term=.6475c26b6a69 and http://www.npr.org/2017/01/31/512439121/trumps-executive-order-on-immigration-annotated all accessed 2 February 2017.

[9] Samuel Huntington, 'The Clash of Civilisations' in *Foreign Affairs* (Summer 1993) 72:3, 22–49.

[10] Anne Salmond. 'Self and Other in Contemporary Anthropology' in Richard Fardon (Ed.) *Counterworks: Managing the Diversity of Knowledge* (London: Routledge, 1995), 23–48.

constructed by White Europeans and North Americans on the basis of an exclusively 'Western' epistemology. Whilst, as Ziauddin Sardar notes, 'Orientalism is an artificial construction,' it has, as Edward Said suggests, been used as the justification for 'Western' hegemony, within both the colonial and postcolonial eras.[11]

Carl Jung suggests that myth is an expression of archetypal themes to be found within our collective unconscious.[12] As a result, whilst a myth may fail to reflect social reality it carries the power to shape our understanding and underpin deeply held assumptions or beliefs. Chiara Bottici makes the point clearly, by 'slipping into our unconsciousness political myths can deeply influence our most fundamental perceptions of the world and thus escape the possibility of critical scrutiny.'[13] When we bear Bottici's observations in mind it becomes easier to understand how the enduring hold of Orientalism and, in the UK, an accompanying myth of Empire provided fertile ground for Samuel Huntington's influential 'clash of civilisations' thesis.

Writing just a few years after the fall of the Berlin Wall in 1989, Huntington asserted that in the aftermath of the Cold War the new geopolitical struggle would revolve around a so-called clash of civilisations rather than political ideologies: 'Conflict between civilizations will be the latest phase in the evolution of conflict in the modern world.'[14] Huntington's thesis reified living cultures and was characterised by the assertion that 'differences among civilisations are not only real; they are basic.'[15] He went further and argued that the next big geo-political struggle would be between what he referred to as 'Western civilisation' and 'Islamic civilisation,' which he depicted in graphically negative terms— 'The crescent-shaped Islamic bloc, from the bulge of Africa to central Asia, has bloody borders.'[16] For Huntington diversity threatened national identity rather than enriching it. Whilst his ideas were widely critiqued the narrative woven by Huntington provided the intellectual camouflage for

---

[11] Ziauddin Sardar, *Orientalism* (Buckingham: Open University Press, 1999), vii and Edward Said, *Orientalism* (London: Penguin Books, 2003 edition), xxii.

[12] Carl Jung, *Archetypes and the Collective Unconscious* (Princeton: Princeton University Press, 1968), 3ff.

[13] Chiara Bottici, 'Towards a Philosophy of Political Myth' in *IRIS—European Journal of Philosophy and Public Debate*, III April 2011, Firenze University Press, 41.

[14] Huntington, op. cit., 22.

[15] Ibid., 25.

[16] Ibid., 35.

the demonising of difference and upsurge of Islamophobia that has characterised life in the postcolonial city for the last 20 years. Huntington implicitly paved the way for the 1997–2010 Labour government's assimilationist community cohesion agenda and foregrounding of so-called British values, the 2010–2015 Conservative government's assertion that multiculturalism has failed and the 2016 British referendum decision to leave the European Union.

Gilroy suggests that this culture of othering reflects a 'post-imperial melancholia'—an ambivalent impotence that has resulted from the loss of Empire, which expresses itself in the demonising of the children, grandchildren and great-grandchildren of its colonial past.[17] Such post-imperial melancholia evidenced itself in the dramatic rise of 'hate-crimes' in the aftermath of the UK's decision to leave the European Union. In a similar vein the 'No Irish, No Blacks, No Dogs' signs in boarding house windows that greeted many Black people migrating to the UK in the 1950s and the 'No More Polish Vermin' flyers handed out in the aftermath of the EU referendum rest on the unholy alliance between the angst-ridden processes of 'othering' and scapegoating.[18]

The objectifying and demonising of Black and Asian-Britons rest on a flawed anthropology, which defines human identity in essentialised binary terms and enables the forging of excluding models of nationhood and belonging whereby particular ethnic or religious groups are defined as threatening cultural outsiders. Such a process of 'othering' provides the raw material upon which the scapegoating of the so-called outsider depends. The Jewish community, the Irish community, the Black community, the Bangladeshi community and, more recently, the Muslim community know what it means to be the scapegoat—to be blamed for society's problems. Robert Beckford argues that the de-humanising and de-valuing of Black people are arguably written into the DNA of Christian history, dating back to the formation of the canonical Gospels.[19] Anthony Reddie and Michael Jagessar highlight the historic nature of the racialised 'othering,' which underpins Britain's post-imperial melancholia, suggesting that 'The construction of the binary of Blackness and Whiteness is a

---

[17] Gilroy, 2004, op. cit., 120.

[18] Web site http://www.bbc.co.uk/news/uk-england-cambridgeshire-36633388 accessed 2 February 2017.

[19] Robert Beckford, *Dread and Pentecostal: A Political Theology for the Black Church in Britain* (London: SPCK, 2000), 68–79.

product of modernity … racialized notions of fixed identity and restricted perspectives on Black human selfhood were the dangerous offspring of the chattel slavery of the Black Atlantic.'[20]

If we are to fashion inclusive urban communities within which plurality and difference are markers of liberative community relations it is vital that we move beyond our addiction to the myth of 'race' upon which the zombies feed. Whilst it has proved to be incredibly difficult to 'kick' our addiction to 'race' only such a shift can enable us to move towards political and theological narratives and social justice movements, which are capable of engaging in a credible manner with our interwoven plurality. Beckford makes the point well, suggesting that 'this multidimensional approach to experience means that liberation strategies will not all be the same because experience is not singular.'[21] A recognition that 'the experience of poor whites within the inner city is similar but also dissimilar from their Indian, Bangladeshi … Caribbean and West African neighbours' can begin to put the zombies back in their box.[22]

RE-INVENTING THE MULTICULTURAL LANDSCAPE

Writing at the beginning of the new millennium Andrew Davey suggested that 'You only have to walk down the streets of any major city to encounter the world.'[23] The postcolonial city is neither singular nor static but dynamic and multiple. Leonie Sandercock is therefore right to remind us that we need to cultivate an 'epistemology of multiplicity' if we are to understand its complexity.[24] Monocultural cul-de-sacs and ring-fenced conceptions of culture, reassuring though they may be, inhibit the forging of genuinely inclusive patterns of citizenship. It is only when we recognise that ethnic and religious diversity is normative rather than exceptional and that identity is plural and fluid that we will begin to overcome the introverted nationalism and resurgent xenophobia that increasingly dominate politics on both sides of the Atlantic.

If we are to wrestle back multiculturalism from political leaders and journalists who present it as a barrier to social cohesion it is important to

[20] Michael N. Jagessar and Anthony G. Reddie, ed. *Black Theology in Britain: A Reader* (London: Equinox, 2007), 10.
[21] Beckford, *Dread and Pentecostal*, 150–151.
[22] Robert Beckford, *God and the Gangs* (London: Darton, Longman & Todd, 2004), 21.
[23] Andrew Davey, *Urban Christianity and Global Order* (London: SPCK, 2001), 4.
[24] Leonie Sandercock, *Towards Cosmopolis* (Chichester: John Wiley & Sons, 1998), 76.

identify the tools and concepts which can help us to fashion an alternative liberative narrative of meaning. A brief examination of the dynamic nature of contemporary diversity, ongoing globalisation processes, criss-crossing patterns of migration and the nature of personal and communal identity can help to provide us with the tools we need to resist the appeal of the zombies, which worried Kant and Beck so much.

Whilst Davey touched upon it and those of us who live in big cities experience it on a daily basis it was the anthropologist Steven Vertovec who first began to theorise what he termed 'superdiversity.'[25] Just as Davey and Vertovec were pointing to our dynamic diversity New Labour government ministers were drawing on the assimilationist community cohesion agenda set by Ted Cantle in their articulation of xenophobic and static definitions of 'Britishness.'[26] Political and academic debate about diversity in the UK has largely framed identity in fixed terms and focused policy and analysis on large settled communities of people of Caribbean and Indian sub-continent heritage. However, as the urban landscape has been transformed it increasingly appears that social policy is framed and research undertaken into a world that is fast disappearing in the rear-view mirror. Vertovec reminds us that even our diversity is diverse. As a result of the confluence of ongoing waves of globalisation and widespread geo-political conflict the twenty-first century has witnessed a movement of people from across the global 'South' to the affluent 'North' not seen for generations. Vertovec argues that, in this context, established ways of thinking about identity fail to respond to the new questions that contemporary migration raises. He suggests that on this new landscape, 'there is much to be gained by a multidimensional perspective on diversity ... and by appreciating the coalescence of factors which condition people's lives.'[27] This new landscape has seen the emergence of plural towns and cities, like Luton and Leicester, where no single ethnic group constitutes a majority of the population.[28] When everybody is part of a minority the identification of so-called British values becomes as difficult as catching water in a net. Such an exercise owes more to essentialist understandings of nation and hege-

---

[25] Steven Vertovec, 'Super-Diversity and Its Implications', *Ethnic and Racial Studies* (2007) 30:6, 1024–1054.

[26] Ted Cantle, *Community Cohesion: A Report of the Independent Review Team* (London: Home Office, 2001).

[27] Vertovec, op. cit., 1026.

[28] Web site http://www.manchester.ac.uk/discover/news/first-plural-towns-and-city-outside-london-revealed accessed 2 February 2017.

monic assimilationist community cohesion agendas than it does to progressive configurations of social inclusion characterised by a commitment to the plurality of British identity.

Vertovec focuses his analysis on patterns of migration. Whilst this has become increasingly important since the onset of the Mediterranean refugee crisis beginning in 2015 an exclusive focus on immigration can perpetuate the misconception that Black and Asian-Britons are cultural outsiders. An obsessive interest in 'the immigrant' can blind us to the new future that is being framed before our eyes. As a result we fail to see the rapid rise of the community of Britons who self-define as people of dual heritage—not just Olympic gold medal winners like Jessica Ennis or Formula 1 world champions like Lewis Hamilton but 1,200,000 Britons in towns and cities across the UK.

This re-invention of identity has the potential to re-frame life in the postcolonial British city in such a way that difference resources a mutually liberative activism capable of forging inclusive models of social cohesion. The life-giving potential of such a new vision of urban life may still be sapped by the zombies that continue to stalk the streets of the postcolonial city. However a critical conversation with aspects of political theology can help us to forge a model of liberative spirituality that is capable of breathing life into the zombie discourse that surrounds diversity. Such a critical conversation, which can only be hinted at here, is vital as we seek to build inclusive post-imperial communities in our superdiverse twenty-first-century cities.

LIFE-GIVING SPIRITUALITIES VERSUS LIFELESS ZOMBIES

The zombie discourse surrounding contemporary multiculturalism, recent British government social policy, excluding narratives of community cohesion, the 'clash of civilisations' thesis and the myth of 'race' upon which they all depend are the products of modernity. I suggest that the intellectual tools of modernity cannot cope with the dynamic and interwoven complexity of the cities of the twenty-first century. In order to forge a new and liberative spirituality we need to move beyond a modernist concern with roots and embrace ways of thinking that focus more on routes—not so much where we are from but how we got here and where we are headed. A critical dialogue with the following theological themes can help us to respond to the zombie discourse surrounding multiculturalism and construct a contextual theologian's tool-kit capable of responding to the challenge.

Catholicity

The scapegoating of Black and Asian-Britons and of the British-Muslim community undermines the central thrust of Christian anthropology, which asserts the interconnected equality of humanity—one people made in the image of the one God. As Kenneth Leech notes, racism and Islamophobia contradict the conviction that all people are 'made in God's image and shine with the divine light.'[29] In the face of the zombie discourse that pervades ongoing policy responses to ethnic and religious diversity, the ancient Christian doctrine of Catholicity has the potential to resource the development of a new and life-giving post-imperial urban spirituality.

Since the Patristic period in Christian history the doctrine of Catholicity has largely been used as a metaphor for the diverse unity of the Church: dispersed across the globe but united around a common faith. The articulation of Catholicity has often focused on orthodox belief as defined by the Nicene Creed in order to identify people as doctrinal 'insiders' and 'outsiders.' In spite of this word of caution I suggest that a re-imagined Catholicity has the potential to resource the development of inclusive and dialogical spiritualities in the postcolonial city, which can begin to drain the life from the zombie discourse which surrounds multiculturalism.

The work of Robert Schreiter provides an important resource for those seeking to re-imagine Catholicity in a globalised world. Schreiter begins by suggesting that the fluid and dynamic nature of contemporary society challenges un-examined discourses about identity, thereby changing the way we view other people and ourselves.[30] Consequently a re-framed dialogical understanding of Catholicity needs to revolve around what Chris Baker has called an 'open-ended and fluid Christology,' which has the flexibility to resource 'blurred encounters' in the superdiverse postcolonial city.[31] For Schreiter such a step is critical, 'For it is in the experience of moving from one place to another ... of negotiating multiple identities ... that insight into where God is at work in a globalized culture will be found.'[32]

[29] Kenneth Leech, *Race: Changing Society and the Churches* (London: SPCK, 2005), 109.

[30] Robert Schreiter, *New Catholicity: Between the Global and the Local* (Maryknoll, NY: Orbis Books, 1997), 15.

[31] Christopher Richard Baker, *The Hybrid Church in the City: Third Space Thinking* (Aldershot: Ashgate, 2007), 146.

[32] Schreiter, op. cit., 59.

In recent years politicians and commentators on the left as well as the right have depicted ever-increasing ethnic and religious diversity as a symptom of social disintegration. Like Gilroy, Modood and Meer, I suggest that such a perspective reflects an *a priori* value judgement about multiculturalism rather than an evidence-based observation.[33] It is possible, and I would argue, vital, to take another view, which frames plurality, movement and dynamic identity as the raw material for liberative and inclusive models of social cohesion. The work of the linguist and postcolonial critic Homi Bhabha can help us in this task.[34] Bhabha speaks of a third space of social discourse—a liminal borderland that is characterised by fluidity, dialogue and the 'blurred encounters' to which Baker refers. As essentialist conceptions of identity rub up against increasingly fluid superdiversity new opportunities for dialogue emerge. Third-space conversations between perceived cultural strangers become the crucible within which new relationships can be forged and new discourses of diversity explored.

A re-framed doctrine of Catholicity, when allied with Schreiter's reflections on movement and multiplicity and the dialogical possibilities of third-space discourse, can begin to subvert the demonising of difference which underpins our cleaving to multicultural zombies. A new Catholicity has the potential to provide a narrative, which can undermine the lingering support for Huntington's 'clash of civilisations' thesis and strengthen those who are struggling 'against those forces in society that, using the signifier of race ... make difference a warrant for discrimination and oppression.'[35] However such a new Catholicity can fulfil its liberative potential only if it is informed by a new conception of the 'common good' within which the marginalised 'stranger' is prioritised.

The Stranger and the Common Good

One of the best known phrases in the Bible is Jesus' commandment in Mark 12:31 to 'love your neighbor as you love yourself.' However it is the far more common biblical injunction to 'welcome the stranger' that can

---

[33] Gilroy, 2004, op. cit., 29 and Nasar Meer & Tariq Modood, 'Cosmopolitanism and Integrationism: Is British Multiculturalism a 'Zombie Category'?' *Identities: Global Studies in Culture and Power* (2014) 21:6, 658–674, 660–661.

[34] Homi K. Bhabha, *The Location of Culture* (London: Routledge, 1994).

[35] Schreiter, op. cit., 95.

more effectively subvert a political and public discourse that demonises the difference that the 'stranger' represents. In 'post-Brexit' Britain and Trump's America where hate-crimes abound, refugee children are left in 'the jungle' bordering Calais and bans on migrants and refugees specifically target people who are Muslim and overwhelmingly non-White, welcoming the 'stranger' represents a prophetic critique of those in power.[36] We are challenged to think again about notions of the 'common good' and to respond to the question that the Teacher of the Law asks Jesus in Luke 10: 'Who is my neighbor?'

The writer of the letter to the Hebrews (13:2) wrote two millennia ago but the challenge of these words echoes down the centuries—'Do not neglect to show hospitality to strangers, for by doing that some have entertained angels without knowing it.'[37] As I have shown above, a toxic narrative surrounding migration, the depiction of multiculturalism as a failed social experiment that fosters segregation and an incipient 'clash of civilisations' culture permeate contemporary British politics. Repeated more than 40 times in the Pentateuch alone, the command to love or welcome the stranger is allied with a commitment to solidarity with the oppressed (Deuteronomy 10:18–19). Its adoption may be costly but this counter-cultural ethic can resource the development of a spirituality which prioritises the demonised stranger and subverts the hegemonic hold of the demonising of difference in the postcolonial city.

Luke Bretherton reminds us that a commitment to welcoming the stranger should not be presented as the 'politically correct' behaviour of progressive Christians. Rather it is a key foundation of Christ-centred spirituality. In his parable about the Day of Judgement in Matthew 25:31–46 Jesus makes it plain that those who welcome the stranger have welcomed him. As Bretherton notes, 'hospitality towards strangers constitutes part of the church's witness to the Christ-event.'[38] However, as welcome as a commitment to hospitality towards the stranger is in the fractured

---

[36] Web sites http://www.bbc.co.uk/news/uk-politics-37640982; https://www.theguardian.com/world/2017/feb/08/dubs-scheme-lone-child-refugees-uk-closed-down?CMP=share_btn_tw and http://www.independent.co.uk/news/world/americas/donald-trump-refugee-ban-executive-order-muslim-majority-countries-syrians-un-united-nations-a7550576.html all accessed 10 February 2017.

[37] *New Revised Standard Version of the Bible* (Oxford: Oxford University Press, 1995), Hebrews 13:2.

[38] Luke Bretherton, *Christianity and Contemporary Politics* (Chichester: Wiley-Blackwell, 2010), 211.

postcolonial city, a word of caution should be raised. When cultural 'insiders' welcome cultural 'outsiders' there is a danger that exclusionary social relations may be re-inforced and binary configurations of 'guest' and 'host' bolstered. If such pitfalls are to be avoided then it is vital that the 'welcoming of the stranger' is permeated by an ethic of mutuality. As Bretherton reminds us 'welcoming the stranger' must revolve around 'a process of decentring and re-orientation to God and neighbour.'[39]

A commitment to 'welcoming the stranger' raises significant hermeneutical questions that must not be side-stepped. Making sense of what we experience and giving it meaning is not a value-free process. We can choose to privilege the meanings that 'insider' power elites attribute to life in the postcolonial city or to listen most closely to marginalised 'outsiders.' Interpreting social reality is never a neutral exercise but is shaped by our experience, our place in society and the values upon which we base our lives. What we see depends on where we are. Consequently the Black accountant in a large church in Birmingham who was told she couldn't be the church treasurer because she couldn't trusted with the collection and the White Church Steward who said this to her recall and give meaning to their encounter in radically different ways. Similarly the White members of a church in London who refused to receive the Body of Christ from the hand of the Church Steward remember the incident in a dramatically different way to the Black Steward who was handing out the bread.

As we seek to defeat the zombies in the postcolonial city the reflections expressed a generation ago by some of the earliest Latin American liberation theologians can come to our aid. God is depicted as being in solidarity with the poor. As Elsa Tamez summarises, 'God identifies himself with the poor to such an extent that the rights of the poor become the rights of God himself.'[40] This intimate relationship between God and the poor moves us beyond an assertion of God's preferential option for the poor to the realisation that the experience of poverty is a place of hermeneutical privilege. The upside-down kingdom, which Jesus articulates, is one that resonates most fully with the left out and the left behind, those who are blessed in Jesus' beatitudes in Matthew 5 and Luke 6. In the face of the physical, psychological and existential damage that racism and Islamophobia continue to do to those whom the included and the powerful frame as

---

[39] Ibid., 360.

[40] Elsa Tamez, *Bible of the Oppressed* (Maryknoll, NY: Orbis Books, 1982), 73. See also Gustavo Gutiérrez, *The Power of the Poor in History* (London: SCM Press, 1983), 131–143.

cultural outsiders, I have argued elsewhere that it is necessary to forge a 'hermeneutics of the demonised,' which subverts insider/outsider divides, 'clash of civilisations' essentialism and hegemonic binary framings of guest and host.[41] A hermeneutics of the demonised outsider demands that we re-think power relations and our understanding of truth, centre and margins. Furthermore when life in Brexit-Britain is viewed through the eyes of the excluded our perception of what constitutes the 'common good' is subverted. When we gaze on the 'common good' from outside and below, dominant perceptions about multiculturalism are disrupted, making it possible to begin to re-imagine a new and liberative theology of the common good that is written by the socially excluded.

The Solidarity of Jesus the 'Cultural Other'

Within a Christian context a re-imagined and enlarged vision of Catholicity and the forging of a counter-hegemonic hermeneutics of the demonised outsider rely upon a model of Christology, which subverts the historic doctrinal dominance of the White Christ. Reddie argues that it is only when we peel away the layers of Eurocentric Christology and embrace the 'otherness' of Jesus the marginalised Palestinian Jew that we will be able to begin constructing a liberative theological narrative capable of resourcing new patterns of faith-based activism, which can challenge the demonising of difference.[42] Whilst he wrote almost a decade before the European refugee crisis, the UK vote to leave the European Union and the so-called Muslim ban by Donald Trump in the USA, Reddie's words retain a powerful contemporary resonance, 'Welcoming the stranger can be a means of grace ... In their very presence we may even see the benevolent presence of the Divine.'[43] Laurie Green also challenges us to recover a liberative Christology of otherness. Jesus, he suggests, 'throws open his Kingdom to those ... considered unclean and of no account, and sets them at the very centre ... Jesus does not simply offer them dispassionate justice but aggressively positive discrimination.'[44]

In the face of the demonising of difference in the postcolonial city and the persistent Orientalism of the 'clash of civilisations' thesis in all its

---

[41] Chris Shannahan, *Voices from the Borderland* (London: Equinox, 2010), 225 and 227.

[42] Anthony G. Reddie, *Working Against the Grain: Re-imaging Black Theology in the 21st Century* (London: Equinox, 2008), 148.

[43] Ibid., 156.

[44] Laurie Green, *Urban Ministry and the Kingdom of God* (London: SPCK, 2003), 85.

populist guises, the articulation of a Christology of liberative difference when aligned with a re-framed Catholicity and the fashioning of a hermeneutics of the demonised can begin to undermine the hegemonic hold of an ethic of oppressive difference. Such a Christology, if it is to be culturally credible, needs to avoid the temptation to re-hash or mimic other, earlier liberative Christologies. Consequently, whilst it is of paramount importance to draw inspiration from figures like Beckford whose articulation of a subversive and emancipatory 'Dread Christ' resonates with historical and contemporary Black experience, it is of critical importance that we draw organically on our own experience of life in the superdiverse but fragmented postcolonial city in order to identify contemporary ontological symbols that have the capacity to articulate a new and culturally resonant Christology of liberation.[45]

With this in mind, as I have argued elsewhere, it is essential that attempts to fashion a Christology of liberative difference in the postcolonial city foreground a critical examination of White identity and normative Whiteness. To date little attempt has been made by White British theologians to begin such an exploration with the exception of Kenneth Leech, who suggests that the articulation of a credible Christology of liberative difference must begin with a critique of the 'edifice of whiteness' and its alignment with a 'history of domination.'[46] If this exploration is to be coherent and persuasive it is essential that White experience in the postcolonial city is not essentialised. Leech, Reddie and Beckford are right to describe Whiteness as a 'location associated with economic privilege.'[47] However the economic social exclusion of sections of the White community, often on impoverished outer city estates, and the resulting existential alienation from mainstream society must not be air-brushed out of the picture because neglecting this experience and this voice will only leave a vacuum, which the far-right will fill with enthusiasm.

The Moral Arc of the Universe…

In the current climate it can often feel as if the demonising of difference has public and political discourse in a death-grip. Such is the hegemonic hold of images of the threatening stranger and the appropriation of multiculturalism by the political class as a synonym for so-called segregation in

[45] Robert Beckford, *Jesus Is Dread* (London: Darton, Longman and Todd, 1998).
[46] Kenneth Leech, 2005. op. cit., 9.
[47] Beckford, 2004, op. cit. *God and the Gangs*, 76.

the postcolonial city that those of us who are determined to articulate an alternative vision of liberative difference can burn out or become completely disillusioned. And yet, I want to persist in arguing that there are reasons to be optimistic, even in the face of the rise of right-wing populism on both sides of the Atlantic.

Writing from a prison cell in Mussolini's Italy the Marxist theorist Antonio Gramsci spoke about what he called the 'cultural war of position'—an ongoing struggle between reactionary and progressive visions of society. Whilst the battle may be long Gramsci insisted that once a seemingly counter-cultural idea gains enough momentum to persuade large sections of a population, the social contract that preserves the status quo can be overcome and a new world brought to birth.[48] We are currently engaged in such a 'cultural war of position.' On one side are the dominant voices within society—government, establishment intellectuals and large sections of the media—those using all the weapons at their disposal to continue to assert the spectre of marauding refugees and migrants posing apocalyptic threats to social cohesion. On the other side are the activists and academics, social movements, community organisers, painters and poets who challenge the hegemony of oppressive difference and assert another, inclusive and egalitarian vision of a society strengthened by its dynamic diversity.

Whilst, as Martin Luther King Jr reminds us, 'the arc of the moral universe bends towards justice' the victory of justice is far from predetermined.[49] If we are to rescue the discourse about multiculturalism in the postcolonial city from the zombie categories that freeze it in time it is vital that a credible and persuasive new narrative is articulated, which uses all of the means at our disposal. As Manuel Castells notes, 'Whoever wins the battle for people's minds will rule, because mighty rigid apparatuses will not be a match in any reasonable timespan for minds mobilised around the power of flexible alternative networks.'[50] If the mobilising of minds around a new discourse of diversity which posits difference as a source of potential liberation rather than as a problem seeking a solution is to be effective, it is essential that we overcome the bunker mentality that can

[48] Anne F. Showstack, *Antonio Gramsci: An Introduction to His Thought* (London: Pluto Press, 1970), 129–204.

[49] Martin Luther King Jr. 'Out of the Long Night' in *The Gospel Messenger* (Elgin; Illinois: The Church of the Brethren, 8 February 1958), 14, column 1.

[50] Manuel Castells, *The Power of Identity: The Information Age...Economy, Society and Culture* (Oxford: Blackwell, 2010), 360.

inhibit activists and academics. A diverse network of reflective practitioners and activist academics is needed if we are to defeat the zombies, which Kant found so frightening. Schreiter's work on what he terms 'local theology' can help us in this task. In his exploration of the emergence of contextual theology in the dying days of Empire Schreiter speaks of theology as a creative partnership between activists and academics. Such an enterprise has the capacity to democratise academy-bound theology and the potential to weave new narratives of meaning that can resource the work of those struggling for social justice.[51]

Wrestling multiculturalism back from the political right, rescuing it from the outmoded zombie categories that no longer reflect the dynamic diversity of the contemporary city and fashioning a counter-hegemonic discourse of liberative difference rely on victory in the 'cultural war of position' to which Gramsci referred. Three interlinked steps on what is likely to be a long journey are necessary if a convincing new discourse of diversity is to take root.

First, it is imperative that the weaving of a new narrative of liberative difference is democratic, inclusive and dialogical. As Schreiter notes contextual theologies belong first and foremost to the communities that give them birth, rather than the academy or the Church—'to allow the professional theologian to dominate … seems to introduce a new hegemony over already oppressed communities.'[52] If we are to supplant the dominance of a culture that demonises difference our conversations must cross often closely guarded ethnic and religious boundaries. Therefore a culturally credible theology of liberative difference in the contemporary postcolonial city must be inherently cross-cultural and inter-faith, as I have argued elsewhere in relation to faith-based community organising in the UK and the USA.[53] Furthermore such a new narrative needs to be characterised by imagination, as ready to listen to the wisdom of the poet and the painter, the song-writer and the story-teller as it is to politicians, professors and preachers.[54]

Second, the myth of academic neutrality must be firmly debunked. Stephen Pattison reminds us that 'Since all theology is human discourse, and all human discourse is conditioned by the socio-political nature of

[51] Robert Schreiter, *Constructing Local Theologies* (Maryknoll, NY: Orbis Books, 1985), 1–21.

[52] Ibid., 19.

[53] Chris Shannahan. *A Theology of Community Organizing—Power to the People* (London/New York: Routledge, 2014).

[54] Schreiter, 1985, op. cit., 18.

reality, all theology must be regarded as biased.'[55] In spite of the protests of those whose vision of the world was shaped by a post-Enlightenment assertion of objectivity there is no neutral research, for neutrality is, in essence, a passive acceptance of the status quo. What then is the job of the intellectual in struggles for liberation in the postcolonial city? In his *Prison Notebooks* Gramsci explores the role of the intellectual, suggesting that historically they have acted as 'the dominant group's "deputies" exercising the subaltern functions of social hegemony.'[56] Writing out of his involvement in the US Civil Rights Movement Cornel West argues that the role of the intellectual is to 'create a vision of the world that puts into the limelight the social misery that is usually hidden or concealed by the dominant viewpoints of a society.'[57] Similarly, Edward Said argues that the academic needs to play a clear and public role in struggles for liberation because 'The purpose of the intellectual's activity is to advance human freedom.'[58] For the pioneer of Latin American liberation theology Gustavo Gutiérrez, 'the theologian is to be an "organic intellectual," a thinker with organic links to the popular liberation undertaking, and with the Christian communities that live their faith by taking this historical task upon themselves as their own.'[59] If incipient Orientalism, cleaving to the reductive 'clash of civilizations' thesis and the consigning of multiculturalism to history are to be defeated ideas matter and that means that academics have a decision to make—Do they remain bystanders or engage as active partners in the struggle against xenophobia, not just in academic journals but in places of worship, community centres and on the street? Do they write about the struggle from a safe distance or, as engaged organic intellectuals, do they feel the 'elemental passions of the people' as Gramsci puts it?[60]

Third, drawing on the work of Paulo Freire, I want to suggest that dialogue, discourse and education need to be seen as essential tools in the struggle to forge a spirituality that can breathe life again into an ailing multiculturalism. In his classic work *Pedagogy of the Oppressed* Freire argues that contextualised and dialogical education can enable people to become

[55] Stephen Pattison, *Pastoral Care and Liberation Theology* (London: SPCK, 1997), 34.

[56] Antonio Gramsci, *Selections from the Prison Notebooks* (London: Lawrence & Wishart, 1971), 12.

[57] Cornel West, *The Cornel West Reader* (New York: Basic Civitas Books, 1999), 551.

[58] Edward Said, *Representations of the Intellectual: The 1993 Reith Lectures* (London: Vintage Press, 1994), 13.

[59] Gustavo Gutierrez, *The Power of the Poor in History* (London: SCM Press, 1983), 103.

[60] Gramsci, 1971, op. cit., 418.

conscious of the nature and cause of their oppression.[61] This 'building of a critical awareness' has a vital role to play if we are to supplant the demonising of difference with an ethic of liberative difference as we strive to build a life after Empire.[62]

As I write the dominant voices in Brexit-Britain and Trump's America appear to be drowning out those who see diversity as strength rather than a 'clear and present danger' to social cohesion. The future feels bleak; perhaps the zombies have gained the upper hand. And yet there are reasons to be optimistic. Amidst the clamour of siren voices loudly asserting the death of multiculturalism the quiet whispers of hope can still be heard that give the lie to the 'othering' of contemporary Orientalism, the ahistorical essentialism of the 'clash of the civilisations' and the demonising of difference. Here are just a few reasons to be hopeful as we try to re-imagine life in the postcolonial city. These stories from early 2017 offer us glimpses of an emerging prophetic critique of xenophobia. In the UK faith leaders held Prime Minister Theresa May to account for her abandonment of Syrian child refugees and her creation of a 'hostile environment' for migrants. In the USA Imam Mohammed Magid challenged the Islamophobia of President Trump at his inter-faith inauguration service at Washington National Cathedral. In Canada hundreds of Jews formed a ring of peace around a mosque in Toronto in the aftermath of the White supremacist attack on a mosque in Quebec. In the USA more than 400 churches publicly committed themselves ready to become places of sanctuary for undocumented migrants and over 100 evangelical Christian leaders took out a full-page advertisement condemning Donald Trump's so-called Muslim ban.[63]

This reclaiming of the prophetic tradition of speaking truth to power offers us some cause for hope. However such activism needs to be allied to a renewed commitment to liberative contextual theological reflection

[61] Paulo Freire, *Pedagogy of the Oppressed* and *Cultural Action for Freedom* (Harmondsworth: Penguin Education, 1972).

[62] Paulo Freire, *Pedagogy of Indignation* (Boulder: Paradigm Publishers, 2004), 66.

[63] Web sites http://iqra.ca/2017/jews-to-form-ring-of-peace-around-toronto-mosque-on-friday/; http://edition.cnn.com/2017/01/20/politics/trump-imam-magid/index.html; https://www.washingtonpost.com/news/acts-of-faith/wp/2017/02/10/franklin-graham-said-immigration-is-not-a-bible-issue-heres-what-the-bible-says/?tid=ss_fb-bottom&utm_term=.120aa9ff2abd; https://www.theguardian.com/commentisfree/2017/feb/12/moral-duty-british-government-help-refugee-children?CMP=share_btn_tw; http://www.independent.co.uk/news/uk/home-news/theresa-may-child-refugees-death-archbishop-canterbury-dubs-accusations-a7574246.html and https://www.washingtonpost.com/news/acts-of-faith/wp/2017/02/08/conservative-evangelicals-join-letter-denouncing-trumps-order-on-refugees/?utm_term=.201c819242a0 all accessed 16 February 2017.

because it is only when we bring progressive social action into a critical dialogue with liberative reflection that it will be possible to win the 'cultural war of position.' One small example of such liberative contextual theological reflection is found in the recent emergence of the cross-cultural and inter-faith 'Faith and Peaceful Relations Forum' in Coventry, which has begun to fashion a dialogical learning community of practitioners, politicians and academics committed to using the resources of faith to build inclusive social cohesion in the 'city of peace and reconciliation.'[64] The battle to defeat the zombies that so worried Kant will be a long one but it can be won.

CONCLUSION

In this chapter I have drawn upon the British experience of resurgent racism in the postcolonial city in order to highlight the pervasive nature of contemporary Orientalism, the 'clash of civilizations' thesis and the scapegoating of people and communities presented as cultural outsiders. The hegemonic grip of this narrative is such that dominant discourses of diversity remain locked into backward-looking debates about identity in a city that is being re-invented before our eyes. This zombie discourse has enabled people with power to assert the so-called death of multiculturalism almost unchallenged.

The intensity of this exclusionary discourse is such that the Trump presidency in the USA and the dawning of Brexit-Britain mark a moment of decision—this is a *Kairos* moment. Will communities of faith move beyond a welcome resurgence in activism to radically re-imagine life after Empire in the postcolonial city? Such a task demands a new theology of liberation that brings the demonising of difference into a critical dialogue with a re-framed vision of Catholicity, a hermeneutics of the demonised, an openness to encountering God in the stranger, an ethic of liberative difference and a vision of Christ the Palestinian outsider. The challenge before us is an enormous one. However there are signs of a new consciousness tentatively emerging and bridges being built from the stones previously used to erect walls. The time has come to put Immanuel Kant out of his misery and defeat the walking dead once and for all. The future of life on the streets of our postcolonial cities depends on us winning the war.

[64] Web site http://fprforum.coventry.ac.uk/ accessed 15 February 2017.

BIBLIOGRAPHY

Baker, Christopher Richard. 2007. *The Hybrid Church in the City: Third Space Thinking*. Aldershot: Ashgate.
Beckford, Robert. 1998. *Jesus Is Dread*. London: Darton, Longman and Todd.
———. 2000. *Dread and Pentecostal: A Political Theology for the Black Church in Britain*. London: SPCK.
———. 2004. *God and the Gangs*. London: Darton, Longman & Todd.
Bottici, Chiara. 2011. Towards a Philosophy of Political Myth. *IRIS—European Journal of Philosophy and Public Debate* III: 31–52.
Bretherton, Luke. 2010. *Christianity and Contemporary Politics*. Chichester: Wiley-Blackwell.
Bruce, Steve. 2002. *God Is Dead: Secularization in the West*. Oxford: Blackwell.
Cantle, Ted. 2001. *Community Cohesion: A Report of the Independent Review Team*. London: Home Office.
Castells, Manuel. 2010. *The Power of Identity: The Information Age...Economy, Society and Culture*. Oxford: Blackwell.
Davey, Andrew. 2001. *Urban Christianity and Global Order*. London: SPCK.
Freire, Paulo. 1972. *Pedagogy of the Oppressed and Cultural Action for Freedom*. Harmondsworth: Penguin Education.
———. 2004. *Pedagogy of Indignation*. Boulder: Paradigm Publishers.
Gilroy, Paul. 2000. *Against Race*. Cambridge, MA: Harvard University Press.
———. 2004. *After Empire: Melancholia or Convivial Culture?* Abingdon: Routledge.
Gramsci, Antonio. 1971. *Selections from the Prison Notebooks*. London: Lawrence & Wishart.
Green, Laurie. 2003. *Urban Ministry and the Kingdom of God*. London: SPCK.
Gutiérrez, Gustavo. 1983. *The Power of the Poor in History*. London: SCM Press.
Huntington, Samuel. 1993. The Clash of Civilisations. *Foreign Affairs* 72 (3): 22–49.
Jagessar, Michael N., and Anthony G. Reddie, eds. 2007. *Black Theology in Britain: A Reader*. London: Equinox.
Jung, Carl. 1968. *Archetypes and the Collective Unconscious*. Princeton: Princeton University Press.
Kant, Immanuel. 1781. *Critique of Pure Reason*. Trans. Kemp Smith, Norman. 1965. New York: St. Martins.
Leech, Leech. 2005. *Race: Changing Society and the Churches*. London: SPCK.
Meer, Nasar, and Tariq Modood. 2014. Cosmopolitanism and Integrationism: Is British Multiculturalism a 'Zombie Category'? *Identities: Global Studies in Culture and Power* 21 (6): 658–674.
New Revised Standard Version of the Bible. 1995. Oxford: Oxford University Press.
Pattison, Stephen. 1997. *Pastoral Care and Liberation Theology*. London: SPCK.

Reddie, Anthony G. 2008. *Working Against the Grain: Re-imaging Black Theology in the 21st Century.* London: Equinox.

Said, Edward. 1994. *Representations of the Intellectual: The 1993 Reith Lectures.* London: Vintage Press.

———. 2003. *Orientalism.* London: Penguin Books.

Salmond, Anne. 1995. Self and Other in Contemporary Anthropology. In *Counterworks: Managing the Diversity of Knowledge*, ed. Richard Fardon, 23–48. London: Routledge.

Sandercock, Leonie. 1998. *Towards Cosmopolis.* Chichester: John Wiley & Sons.

Sardar, Ziauddin. 1999. *Orientalism.* Buckingham: Open University Press.

Schreiter, Robert. 1985. *Constructing Local Theologies.* Maryknoll, NY: Orbis Books.

———. 1997. *New Catholicity: Between the Global and the Local.* Maryknoll, NY: Orbis Books.

Shannahan, Chris. 2010. *Voices from the Borderland: Re-imagining Cross-cultural Urban Theology in the 21st Century.* London: Equinox.

———. 2014. *A Theology of Community Organizing—Power to the People.* London/New York: Routledge.

Showstack, Anne F. 1970. *Antonio Gramsci: An Introduction to His Thought.* London: Pluto Press.

Slater, John, and George Ritzer. 2001. Interview with Ulrich Beck. *Journal of Consumer Culture* 1 (2): 261–277.

Tamez, Elsa. 1982. *Bible of the Oppressed.* Maryknoll, NY: Orbis Books.

Vertovec, Steven. 2007. Superdiversity and Its Implications. *Ethnic and Racial Studies* 30 (6): 1024–1054.

Ward, Graham, and Michael Hoelzl, eds. 2008. *The New Visibility of Religion: Studies in Religion and Cultural Hermeneutics.* London: Continuum.

West, Cornel. 1999. *The Cornel West Reader.* New York: Basic Civitas Books.

SUBJECT INDEX[1]

[1] Note: Page numbers followed by 'n' refer to notes.

© The Author(s) 2019
J. Dunn et al. (eds.), *Multiple Faiths in Postcolonial Cities*, Postcolonialism and Religions,
https://doi.org/10.1007/978-3-030-17144-5

Place Index[1]

[1] Note: Page numbers followed by 'n' refer to notes.

© The Author(s) 2019
J. Dunn et al. (eds.), *Multiple Faiths in Postcolonial
Cities*, Postcolonialism and Religions,
https://doi.org/10.1007/978-3-030-17144-5

Rusholme, 15n1, 16, 16n2, 22,
26, 28, 31
United States of America
Boston MA, 39
Carbondale IL, 46
Colorado Springs CO, 39

Houston TX, 40
New York NY, 40

Y
Yemen, 133

People Index

A
Akoth, Jane, 12, 87–108
Antonio, Edward, 4, 11
Augustine, 128

B
Bonhoeffer, Dietrich, 12, 109–128
Brett, Mark, vi
Buddha, 37

C
Christ, Jesus, 37, 58, 59, 68–71, 104,
  112, 114, 116–128
Chung, Paul S., 10
Confucius, 37
Cox, Harvey, 128
Cox, Jo, 32

E
Ennis-Hill, Jessica, 138

F
Freire, Paulo, 147

G
Gramsci, Antonio,
  145–147
Gutiérrez, Gustavo, 147

H
Habermas, Jürgen, 113
Hamilton, Lewis, 138
Heaney, Robert, 7

I
Ignatieff, Michael, 60

J
Joy, David, vi,
  12, 13

© The Author(s) 2019
J. Dunn et al. (eds.), *Multiple Faiths in Postcolonial
Cities*, Postcolonialism and Religions,
https://doi.org/10.1007/978-3-030-17144-5